Chai

Learning for Jewish Life

Parent Education

by Barbara Binder Kadden

URJ Press
New York, New York

Printed on acid-free paper

Manufactured in the United States of America
10 9 8 7 6 5 4 3 2 1

Development of the
CHAI: Learning for Jewish Life curriculum
has been made possible in part
by the generous support of the
Gilbert Tilles Endowment Fund.

Additional funding has been provided by the
Feldman Library Fund, a gift of the
Milton and Sally Feldman Foundation
in memory of Sally Feldman.

Contributors

Alan J. Levin, Ph.D. *Project Director*
Joanne Doades, M.A.R.E. *Assistant Director for Curriculum Development, Department of Lifelong Jewish Learning*
Michael H. Goldberg *Project Editor*
Wendy Rapport, RJE *Associate Director, Department of Lifelong Jewish Learning*
Faye Tillis Lewy, z"l *Project Consultant*

Authors

Michelle Shapiro Abraham, MAJE, RJE *Family Education*
Keren Alpert *Temple Boards and Education Committee Guides*
Lisa Lieberman Barzilai, MAJE, RJE *Curriculum Core*
Irene Bolton *Curriculum Core*
Joanne Doades, M.A.R.E. *Early Childhood Parent Education, Curriculum Core*
Deborah Gettes *Curriculum Core*
Melanie Cole Goldberg, MAJE, MAJCS, RJE *Curriculum Core*
Debbie Joseph *Curriculum Core*
Barbara Binder Kadden, MAJE, MAJCS, RJE *Parent Education*
Martha Katz, M.A. *Early Childhood Parent Education*
Alan J. Levin, Ph.D. *Early Childhood Parent Education*
Lesley Litman, M.A. *Curriculum Core*
Marlene Myerson, MEd, RJE *Curriculum Core*
Deborah Niederman, MAJE, RJE *Curriculum Core*
Renee B. Rittner, MAJE, MSW *Teacher Training*
Cheri Ellowitz Silver, MAJE, MAJCS, M.S.Ed., RJE *Mitkadem Hebrew Program*
Lesley Silverstone, MAJE, RJE *Teacher Training*

Academic Advisors

Isa Aron, Ph.D., RJE *Teacher Training*
Lisa Grant, Ph.D. *Parent Education*
Rabbi Sam Joseph, RJE *Temple Boards, Education Committee Guides, Curriculum Core*
Jo Kay, M.A. *Family Education, Early Childhood Parent Education, Curriculum Core*
Sara Lee, MAJE, M.S.Ed., RJE *Mitkadem Hebrew Program*
Michael Zeldin, Ph.D, RJE *Curriculum Core*

NATE Readers

Lori L. Abramson, MAJE, RJE
Judith V. Aronson, MTS, RJE
Birgit R. Anderson, MAJE, RJE
Tirza Arad
Alan D. Bennett, FRE, RJE
Deena Bloomstone, MAJE, RJE
Sherry Blumberg, Ph.D., RJE
Debra Colodny
Mindy B. Davids, MAJE, RJE
Itzik Eshel, Ph.D.
Robin Eisenberg, MEd, RJE
Terri Ginsburg, MEd
Abra Greenspan
Sharon Halper
Rabbi Vered Harris, MAJE
Ava Keenen, MEd
Julie Lambert, MAJE, RJE
Deborah Niederman, MAJE, RJE
Fran Pearlman, M.A., RJE
Sandy Robbins, MSJS, RJE
Roslyn Roucher, MAJE, RJE
Mona Senkfor, RJE
Debra Siroka, MEd, RJE
Anne Stein
Rabbi Peretz Wolf-Prusan

Table of Contents

G'milut Chasadim

Introduction

A home is built by wisdom,
And is established by understanding;
By knowledge are its rooms filled
With all precious and beautiful things. (Proverbs 24:4)

The core of Jewish life lies within the Jewish home. As educators, rabbis, teachers, and community leaders, we have an obligation and responsibility to help develop and nurture the Judaism of our congregants. This in turn will affect and strengthen the Judaism that is lived and learned by the children of our congregants. Jewish parenting education is crucial because it empowers parents to be the key to the Jewish identity and values of their children. Parents have varying levels of Jewish knowledge and they do not always know how to transmit that knowledge to their children. The CHAI Parent Education sessions are intended to educate, empower, and influence the parents—who are our partners in the Jewish education of their children—to feel more at home with being Jewish, to make Judaism more meaningful, and to bring that meaning into their lives and ultimately into the lives of their children.

The Parent Education component of the CHAI curriculum is comprised of eighteen sessions, divided into three categories—Torah, *Avodah*, and *G'milut Chasadim*—of six sessions each. The sessions run approximately ninety fully-packed minutes. Depending on the group, the facilitator may need to edit the number of discussion questions utilized during the session if it is necessary to keep the sessions to exactly ninety minutes.

The eighteen sessions cover a wide range of topics:

Torah

- *V'shinantam L'vanecha:* **And You Shall Teach Your Children** has parents examine their attitudes, beliefs, and commitment to the Jewish education of themselves and their children.

- **Bless Me, Too: Parental Favoritism and Sibling Rivalry in the Bible** utilizes excerpts from the Torah portion *Toldot* to examine the issues of parental favoritism and sibling rivalry.

- **Parenting Jewish Children (For Parents Who Are Non-Jews, Jewish by Choice, or Jewish by Birth)** engages parents in dialogue and conversation on issues that directly affect our interfaith families.

- *V'higaditah L'vanecha:* **You Shall Tell Your Child on That Day** includes basic study of the holiday of Passover and how to choose a Haggadah. A take-home resource handbook for the celebration of Passover is included with the session materials.

- **The Land of Israel: Exploring Our Connection, Connecting Our Children** focuses on the enduring connection between the Jewish people and Israel, the Promised Land.

- **What the Four Children of the Passover Seder Can Teach Us About Parenting** uses study of the biblical verses that are the basis of the story of the Four Children along with rabbinic commentary to teach us about the personalities of the Four Children and the implication of the story for our own parenting.

Avodah

- **Shabbat: Day of Rest, Day of Wonder, Day of Peace** focuses on the meaning of Shabbat in Jewish life and in the lives of the session participants. A take-home issue of "The Jewish Parent Page" for Shabbat is included with the session materials.

- **Blessing Our Children: Building Connection, Building Love** teaches parents the background, meaning, and ritual of blessing one's children.

- **Making the Connection: The Power of Jewish Ritual** examines the meaning, purpose, and importance of ritual in Jewish life.

- **One Hundred Blessings Every Day** reminds us that Jewish tradition encourages us to say one hundred blessings every day. How we can incorporate blessings into our daily lives and what this means for our families is the focus of this session.

- **With These Words: God, Spirituality, Prayer, and Parenting** guides parents in developing a comfort level to talk about God, spirituality, and prayer with their children.

- **Thirteen Steps on the Path of Jewish Beliefs, Values, and Ethics** is an exploration of the guiding principles of Jewish life as found in the *Amidah,* the central prayer of Jewish worship.

G'milut Chasadim

- **Sacred Obligations: Discovering Meaning in the Mitzvot** asks the participants to reflect on the mitzvah choices they have made, the influence their observance has had on themselves and their children, and new mitzvot they may want to observe.

- ***Havdalah:* Reaching for the Sacred** encourages the participants to bring sacred time into every day of their lives and the life of their family, just as the sweet smelling spices of *Havdalah* carry us into the new week.

- ***Sh'lom Bayit:* Creating a Shelter of Peace** teaches the Jewish value of *sh'lom bayit,* peaceful and loving homes.

- **Sustaining the World through Torah, Worship, and Deeds of Loving-Kindness** is devoted to exploring the concepts of Torah, *avodah,* and *g'milut chasadim.*

- **Difference Can Be Our Strength: Becoming a Welcoming Community** focuses on the role of parents in responding to diversity and difference in the Jewish community.

- **Parenting Is *Tikkun Olam*** pairs the concept of *tikkun olam*—the restoration or repair of an incomplete world—with Jewish parenting and asks the question, Is it possible to repair our world through the parenting of our children?

Suggestions for Implementing the Parent Education Sessions

Outreach

In addition to announcements from the pulpit and temple bulletin articles about the parent education sessions, many prospective participants respond positively to personal invitations to attend sessions. These invitations may be extended in person, when a parent is at the synagogue, or by telephone. Reminders sent via email or phone are also helpful a day or two prior to the program.

Follow-up

Sending an email or postcard or making a phone call after a program thanking individuals for participating demonstrates an appreciation for their attendance. Additionally, it emphasizes the desire on the part of the congregation to strengthen connections with members.

Environment

A warm and welcoming environment is essential to the success of a program. It is important that the session facilitator be welcoming and nonjudgmental of the attendees. This helps ensure that they are comfortable participating in the program and sharing in the discussions. Providing some refreshments in a clean, well-lighted, and organized space with adequate and appropriate seating are elements that create the appropriate physical environment. Giving participants nametags will help the facilitator and participants address each other on a first name basis. The facilitator may want to begin each session by reciting with the participants the blessing said before the study of Torah:

> בָּרוּךְ אַתָּה יי אֱלֹהֵינוּ מֶלֶךְ הָעוֹלָם אֲשֶׁר קִדְּשָׁנוּ בְּמִצְוֹתָיו וְצִוָּנוּ לַעֲסוֹק בְּדִבְרֵי תוֹרָה.
>
> *Baruch atah Adonai, Eloheinu Melech haolam, asher kid'shanu b'mitzvotav v'tzivanu la'asok b'divrei Torah.*
>
> We praise You, Eternal God, Sovereign of the universe, who calls us to holiness through mitzvot, commanding us to engage in the study of Torah.

The Facilitator

It is crucial that the facilitator be completely familiar with the session that she or he intends to present. It is essential that the facilitator thoroughly reads through the session, understands it, and assembles the appropriate materials to help ensure the success of the presentation. In addition to the rationale and intent of the session, a materials list, texts for duplication, and specific directions for implementing the session are given. The Parent Education sessions should be led by an individual who has some background in group facilitation as well as some Judaic literacy. The facilitator could be a lay leader, teacher, or synagogue professional (educator, rabbi, cantor).

Family Diversity

As the facilitator, you may be welcoming parents who are in a traditional, two-parent family with a mother and father; or the family may have two mothers or two fathers or a single parent; or the family may include adoptive parents and/or interfaith parents. Additionally, grandparents or other relatives may be fulfilling the parental role. It is important for the facilitator to recognize that families come in many different constructs, and to be alert and sensitive to this diversity.

Curriculum Methodology—Understanding by Design

As a part of the *CHAI: Learning for Jewish Life* curriculum initiative, the Parent Education sessions have been developed using the curricular model called *Understanding by Design.* Four key terms that appear in the introduction to each session are defined below:

- *Enduring Understanding*—A statement of the core values upon which the parent education sessions are based.
- *Essential Questions*—The guiding questions used by the curriculum writer in developing the parent education sessions.
- *Questions to Be Addressed*—Specific questions addressed within the context of the session.
- *Evidence of Understanding*—Written or verbal statements, or changes in behavior, that demonstrate that the learning has occurred. The evidence of understanding indicates the effectiveness of the session.

The majority of the Parent Education sessions include a take-home component to extend the learning that has taken place during the session and bring it directly into the homes of the participants.

It is our hope that through these sessions the participants will be able to fulfill the words of this blessing in their own homes:

> *May this home be a place of happiness and health, creativity and kindness.*
> *May all who visit and live here know only blessing and peace.*

Torah Session 1
V'shinantam L'vanecha:
And You Shall Teach Your Children

Introduction

Judaism calls upon parents not only to teach their children but also to teach themselves. For many, formal Jewish education ends when one becomes a bar or bat mitzvah. Truthfully, that life cycle event is not the end of the process but rather a beginning. This session asks parents to examine their attitudes, beliefs, and commitment to the religious education of themselves and of their children. The concluding activity in the session asks parents to create a Jewish education ethical will. You may want to refer to *G'milut Chasadim* Lesson 3 in the *CHAI Level 5 Curriculum Core* for examples of ethical wills.

Enduring Understanding

Nurturing a strong Jewish identity requires the active participation of parents in their children's Jewish living and learning experiences.

Essential Questions

1. Who am I as a Jewish parent and a Jewish role model?

2. How does one establish a sacred relationship between parent and child?

3. What makes a meaningful Jewish life?

4. What does it mean to be a Jewish family?

Questions to Be Addressed

1. Why does Judaism place responsibility for the Jewish education of children on their parents?

2. Why should a Jewish individual continually educate himself or herself?

3. What are a parent's obligations and responsibilities concerning a child's Jewish education?

Evidence of Understanding

- Participants will identify core personal beliefs about Jewish education as it relates to themselves and their children.
- Participants will read and respond to Jewish texts on the subject of Jewish education.
- Participants will write a Jewish education "ethical will" for their children.

Session Overview

- Set Induction (15–20 minutes)
- Text Study (40–45 minutes)
- Conclusion (20–30 minutes)

Materials Needed

- Photocopies of all text, discussion, and take-home materials (pages 4–8)
- Blank 3" x 5" Post-it notes
- Pens
- A large sheet of poster board labeled "Jewish education should be:"
- A second sheet of poster board labeled "My responsibilities for my child's Jewish education are:"
- A third sheet of poster board labeled "My responsibilities for my Jewish education are:"

SESSION PLAN

Set Induction (15–20 minutes)

1. Distribute copies of the handouts on pages 4–8. Ask for one volunteer to read The Importance of Jewish Education on page 4 aloud.
2. Ask each participant to write responses to the open-ended questions that appear on the three posters:
   - Jewish education should be:
   - My responsibilities for my child's Jewish education are:
   - My responsibilities for my Jewish education are:

   Have participants write their responses on Post-it notes and place them on the appropriate posters. When the writing is complete, read the responses aloud. Participants will revisit these responses at the end of the session.

Text Study (40–45 minutes)

1. Divide the participants into small discussion groups of approximately seven to ten people per group. Ask the groups to read the texts and discuss the questions on pages 5–7. Ask for a volunteer leader to help facilitate the discussion in each group.

2. After the discussions, reconvene as one group and ask the participants to share any new thoughts, ideas, and feelings they now have about Jewish education.

Conclusion (20–30 minutes)

1. Ask participants to reconsider their responses to the questions posed in the posters at the beginning of the session. Based on what they learned today, would they change any of their responses?

2. Explain to participants that since biblical times, it has been Jewish tradition to create an ethical will as a way to concretely impart values and ethics to future generations. Even while they are alive and well, however, this model can help parents explain to their children the goals, values, and meanings they associate with providing their children with a Jewish education. Ask participants to complete the Jewish Education Ethical Will letter on page 8 and talk about its contents with their children. Invite parents to create their own letters if they so choose.

The Importance of Jewish Education

With the fall of the Second Temple in Jerusalem and the rise of rabbinic Judaism, academies of learning and schools were established. The Rabbis created a system of universal Torah study. There was concern that all children should have the opportunity to learn. Whether or not they had parents, the community took on the responsibility of educating the young. According to the Talmud, one was not to move to a town that did not have a teacher. Another teaching from the Talmud tells us that the world endures only because of the breath of school children.

Text Study

Text 1

You shall love Adonai *your God with all your mind, with all your strength, with all your being. Set these words, which I command you this day, upon your heart. Teach them faithfully to your children; speak of them in your home and on your way, when you lie down and when you rise up. Bind them as a sign upon your hand; let them be a symbol before your eyes; inscribe them on the doorposts of your house, and on your gates.*

(*V'AHAVTA:* DEUTERONOMY 6:5–9)

Text 2

[Rabbi] Judah said in the name of Rav: The name of that man, Joshua ben Gamla, should always be mentioned on good occasions. But for him, the Torah would have been forgotten in Israel. Formerly, if a child had a [living] father, his father taught him Torah; if he had no father, he did not learn Torah. . . . it was ordained that teachers of young children should be set up in Jerusalem. . . . Even so, if a child had a father, the father would take him up to Jerusalem and have him taught; if he had no father, the child would not go up and study. Then it was ordained that teachers of youths be set up in each district and that youths enter school at the age of sixteen or seventeen. But when a teacher was annoyed with one of them, that one would rebel against the teacher and leave school. So Joshua ben Gamla came along and ordained that teachers of little children be set up in each district and in each town, and that children enter school at the age of six or seven.

(BABYLONIAN TALMUD *BAVA BATRA* 21A, IN HAYIM NAHMAN BIALIK AND YEHOSHUA HANA RAVINTZKY, EDS., *THE BOOK OF LEGENDS/SEFER HA-AGGADAH,* TRANS. WILLIAM G. BRAUNDE [NEW YORK: SCHOCKEN BOOKS, 1992], PP. 416–471)

Text 3

It is the responsibility of parents to teach Torah to their children. The synagogue and the school are indispensable means to this end, and the community bears the obligation of providing for these institutions and for the training of teachers and other educational specialists. But the child's essential religious and moral development occurs at home, based upon values established and exemplified by his or her parent(s). It is therefore incumbent upon parents to insure that there will be a truly and unmistakably Jewish household. Home rituals, such as blessings recited over the meal and Shabbat and holiday observance, are the core of Jewish life and ought to be experienced as such in the Jewish home. It is a mitzvah to set aside time for daily prayer. When there are no services at the synagogue or if one cannot attend the synagogue, the home is a perfectly appropriate place for the prayer service. A Jewish home should have a Jewish library, and time should be set aside for regular Torah study.

(MARK WASHOFSKY, *JEWISH LIVING: A GUIDE TO CONTEMPORARY REFORM PRACTICE* [NEW YORK: UAHC PRESS, 2001])

Questions for Discussion

1. What do these texts, both ancient and modern, tell us about the responsibility of parents and of the community in relation to educating children?

2. How does Rabbi Washofsky's statement synthesize the values presented in the *V'ahavta* and the Talmud excerpt?

3. Why do you send your child to religious school and Hebrew school? What do you hope the outcome will be?

4. How do we now best provide for the Jewish education of our children? What part is our responsibility and what part is the responsibility of the community?

5. In what ways do we need to educate ourselves Jewishly as adults? What effect or influence might our commitment to personal Jewish education have on our children?

6. Brainstorm with the group ways in which parents can become their child's primary educator, how they can model Jewish learning, and how they can be supportive of their child's education.

Jewish Education Ethical Will

Dear ____________________________,

These are my hopes and dreams for your Jewish education:

It is important to me that you receive a Jewish education because:

It is important to the Jewish community that you receive a Jewish education because:

When you complete your Jewish education I would like you to know:

And I hope you will:

I am here to help you build Jewish memories and Jewish values. These are things that I want us to do (or continue to do) together:

I plan to do the following to help you grow as a Jew:

And for myself I plan to do the following for my own Jewish growth and development:

With love,

Torah Session 2
Bless Me, Too: Parental Favoritism and Sibling Rivalry in the Bible

INTRODUCTION

"Bless me, too," Esau cries to his father, Isaac, when Esau discovers that his brother, Jacob, has stolen the blessing that is Esau's birthright. This session focuses on the question of how to be a fair and just parent when there is more than one child in the family. Utilizing text excerpts from the Torah portion *Toldot,* participants study the issues of parental favoritism and sibling rivalry both in the original biblical context and as they relate to contemporary families. Two Torah texts and one contemporary text with accompanying questions are included in this session. This session is organized as *chevruta* study along with group discussion. *Chevruta* is a traditional Jewish study system in which two people learn together, essentially mentoring each other through the study process. It would be advantageous to set up tables so that *chevruta* partners can sit across from each other for paired study, yet the group is physically close enough to switch smoothly to large group discussion. In the course of this session, the presenter will be creating a written record on a chalkboard or on poster board or paper of the participant responses to the phrase "Good parenting is ____________," along with their responses to the group discussion questions. Additionally, the Essential Questions are to be displayed. The focus of the Summary and Synthesis discussion will be this side-by-side presentation as it relates to parental responsibilities.

Note that although the Torah texts needed for this session are included and may be distributed to participants, it would be preferable to provide copies of the Torah (such as *The Torah: A Modern Commentary,* ed. W. Gunther Plaut [New York: URJ Press, 2004]) in order for participants to have a more authentic Torah study experience.

ENDURING UNDERSTANDING

Nurturing a strong Jewish identity requires the active participation of parents in their children's Jewish living and learning experiences.

ESSENTIAL QUESTIONS

1. Who am I as a Jewish parent and a Jewish role model?
2. How does one establish a sacred relationship between parent and child?
3. What makes a meaningful Jewish life?
4. What does it mean to be a Jewish family?

Questions to Be Addressed

1. How can the study of Jewish texts help me find the answers to issues I face as a parent?
2. How can ancient Jewish texts relate to contemporary Jewish life?

Evidence of Understanding

- Participants will complete the statement "Good parenting is ___________."
- Participants will compare and discuss the responses to the initial statement "Good parenting is ___________" in light of their Torah study session and the Essential Questions.

Materials Needed

- Photocopies of the text materials and the accompanying discussion questions (pages 12–18)
- Chalkboard and chalk or flip chart and markers

Session Overview

- Set Induction (10 minutes)
- Text Study and Discussion (40 minutes)
- Summary and Synthesis (10 minutes)
- Parenting Siblings Today (10 minutes)
- Conclusion (10 minutes)

SESSION PLAN

Set Induction (10 minutes)

1. Explain to participants that in this session they will be looking at the topic of sibling rivalry in the Torah and in their own experiences as parents.
2. Ask the participants to complete the following statement with a one word response:

   Good parenting is ___________________.

   Record participant responses on the board or flip chart.

   Display the Essential Questions (page 16) next to the participant responses to the "Good parenting" statement. Explain that you will be returning to this material at the end of the session.

Text Study and Discussion (40 minutes)

1. Divide the participants into *chevruta* study pairs. If there is not an even number of participants, create one group of three.

2. Hand out the texts and questions on pages 12–18 and instruct the *chevruta* pairings to read Text 1 and use the *Chevruta* Discussion Questions as the focus of their conversation. Inform the pairs that they have 10 minutes to read and discuss the first text, after which the whole group will discuss it.

3. After 10 minutes have elapsed, ask the participants to reconvene as one group. Lead a discussion using the Group Discussion Questions. Record participant responses to the Group Discussion Questions on the board or flip chart. Try to keep the group discussion to 10 minutes.

4. Repeat this process for Text 2.

Summary and Synthesis (10 minutes)

The purpose of the summary discussion is for the participants to synthesize the new lessons they have learned from the text study with their personal views on parenting and to apply that learning to issues they face in parenting.

Ask the participants to review the Essential Questions, the responses to the statement "Good parenting is ______," and the responses to the Group Discussion Questions from the text excerpts they studied. Then discuss the following questions:

- What issues did the biblical texts raise about parenting?
- Did the text study and discussion help you find answers to issues that you face as a parent? If you are comfortable, share and describe those issues.

Parenting Siblings Today (10 minutes)

1. Ask a volunteer to read the text on page 17 aloud for the group.

2. Discuss the following questions:
   - What is your reaction to Rabbi Cohen's observations about sibling relationships?
   - After studying the story of Jacob and Esau, can you identify one or two ways in which you might be more sensitive to your children's differing needs in the future?

Conclusion (10 minutes)

1. Ask participants to turn to Suggestions for Parenting Siblings on page 18 and review it with the group. Ask participants to comment on any of the points that they have a strong reaction to.

2. Review the responses to "Good parenting is ________" that you have referred to from the beginning of the session. Ask for comments about changes in feelings on the subject since the session began.

3. If it is possible to offer an ongoing Jewish parenting study or discussion group at your synagogue, you may want to see if there is interest in scheduling additional sessions.

Text Study and Discussion

Text 1

This is the story of Isaac, son of Abraham. Abraham begot Isaac. Isaac was forty years old when he took to wife Rebekah, daughter of Bethuel the Aramean of Paddan-aram, sister of Laban the Aramean. Isaac pleaded with Adonai *on behalf of his wife, because she was barren; and* Adonai *responded to his plea, and his wife Rebekah conceived. But the children struggled in her womb, and she said, "If so, why do I exist?" She went to inquire of* Adonai, *and* Adonai *answered her, "Two nations are in your womb, Two separate peoples shall issue from your body; One people shall be mightier than the other, And the older shall serve the younger." When her time to give birth was at hand, there were twins in her womb. The first one emerged red, like a hairy mantle all over; so they named him Esau. Then his brother emerged, holding on to the heel of Esau; so they named him Jacob.*[1] *Isaac was sixty years old when they were born.*

When the boys grew up, Esau became a skillful hunter, a man of the outdoors; but Jacob was a mild man, who stayed in camp. Isaac favored Esau because he had a taste for game; but Rebekah favored Jacob. Once when Jacob was cooking a stew, Esau came in from the open, famished. And Esau said to Jacob, "Give me some of that red stuff to gulp down, for I am famished"—which is why he was named Edom. Jacob said, "First sell me your birthright." And Esau said, "I am at the point of death, so of what use is my birthright to me?" But Jacob said, "Swear to me first." So he swore to him and sold his birthright to Jacob. Jacob then gave Esau bread and lentil stew; and he ate and drank, and he rose and went away. Thus did Esau spurn his birthright.

(GENESIS 25:19–34)

[1]Esau (עֵשָׂו *Eisav* in Hebrew) may be related to the Arabic word *av'tha,* thick-haired. Jacob (יַעֲקֹב *Ya'akov* in Hebrew) is a word play on עָקֵב *akeiv,* heel. See W. Gunther Plaut, ed., *The Torah: A Modern Commentary* (New York: UAHC Press, 1981), p. 173.

Chevruta Discussion Questions

1. Did Isaac and Rebekah want children? What is the evidence for that?
2. What information did Rebekah learn about her children?
3. Do you think that information could affect the way she felt about her children? If so, in what ways might she be influenced?

Group Discussion Questions

1. What influences the way you think about your children?
2. Can you recognize traits and characteristics in your children common in your family or in that of your spouse? Do these traits and characteristics affect the way you relate to your children?
3. *Kadosh* means holy, but it also carries the connotation of unique or special. Given the stresses and strains of daily life, how can one focus on the uniqueness and holiness of one's children? How does this focus help build confidence and self-esteem in a child? In a family?
4. To what extent do you think a parent is responsible for the actions of a child? Until what agc?

Text 2

When Isaac was old and his eyes were too dim to see he called his older son Esau and said to him, "My son." He answered, "Here I am." And he said, "I am old now, and I do not know how soon I may die. Take your gear, your quiver and bow, and go out into the open and hunt me some game. Then prepare a dish for me such as I like, and bring it to me to eat, so that I may give you my innermost blessing before I die." Rebekah had been listening as Isaac spoke to his son Esau. When Esau had gone out into the open to hunt game to bring home, Rebekah said to her son Jacob, "I overheard your father speaking to your brother Esau, saying, 'Bring me some game and prepare a dish for me to eat, that I may bless you, with Adonai*'s approval, before I die.' Now, my son, listen carefully as I instruct* *you. Go to the flock and fetch me two choice kids, and I will make of them a dish for your father, such as he likes. Then take it to your father to eat, in order that he may bless you before he dies." Jacob answered his mother Rebekah, "But my brother Esau is a hairy man and I am smooth-skinned. If my father touches me, I shall appear to him as a trickster and bring upon myself a curse, not a blessing." But his mother said to him, "Your curse, my son, be upon me! Just do as I say and go fetch them for me." He got them and brought them to his mother, and his mother prepared a dish such as his father liked. Rebekah then took the best clothes of her older son Esau, which were there in the house, and had her younger son Jacob put them on; and she covered his hands and the hairless part of his neck with the skins of the kids. Then she put in the hands of her son Jacob the dish and the bread that she had prepared.*

(GENESIS 27:1–17)

Notes:

Jacob manages to convince his father that he is Esau and receives the blessing intended for his older brother. Esau is heartbroken to learn that his blessing has been taken and cries out to his father, asking if his father has only one blessing to bestow (Genesis 27:18–40).

Some commentators have interpreted that Isaac was not fooled by Jacob's deception, but simply went along with it because he realized that Jacob was the more appropriate inheritor of the blessing and he [Isaac] did not have the courage to face Esau with this knowledge. (For more, see W. Gunther Plaut, ed., *The Torah: A Modern Commentary* [New York: UAHC Press, 1981], p. 190.)

The blessing Jacob received from his father Isaac:

"May God give you / Of the dew of heaven and the fat of the earth, / Abundance of new grain and wine. / Let peoples serve you, / And nations bow to you; / Be master over your brothers, / And let your mother's sons bow to you. / Cursed be they who curse you, / Blessed they who bless you."

(GENESIS 27:28–29)

The blessing Esau received from his father Isaac:

"See, your abode shall enjoy the fat of the earth / And the dew of heaven above. / Yet by your sword you shall live, / And you shall serve your brother; / But when you grow restive, / You shall break his yoke from your neck."

(GENESIS 27:39–40)

Chevruta Discussion Questions

1. Do you think Isaac and Rebekah's parenting styles complement each other or are they at odds?

2. With what did Isaac bless each of his sons? How do you think these blessings may have affected the relationship between the brothers?

Group Discussion Questions

1. After reviewing the biblical texts, how might you define good parenting? *(The facilitator should record these answers on the "Good parenting is____" chart set up earlier.)*

2. Is it possible to parent children equally or is it human nature to prefer one child over another?

3. With what do you want your children blessed?

4. Is it in your ability to see that those blessings are fulfilled? Explain.

Essential Questions

1. Who am I as a Jewish parent and a Jewish role model?
2. How does one establish a sacred relationship between parent and child?
3. What makes a meaningful Jewish life?
4. What does it mean to be a Jewish family?

Parenting Siblings Today

Even today we parents sometimes inflame the relationships among our children by the way we treat them and show our affection. Even when we try to be even-handed, children sometimes feel we are not as close to them as we are to a brother or sister, and then, who better to take out their frustrations on than the object of their jealousy? . . . This is the challenge that parents face every day if we are blessed with more than one child or are part of an extended blended family. Even though we may have somewhat different feelings for each of our children and stepchildren, can we respond in a meaningful way to each one?

(RABBI NORMAN J. COHEN, *SELF, STRUGGLE AND CHANGE: FAMILY CONFLICT STORIES IN GENESIS AND THEIR HEALING INSIGHTS FOR OUR LIVES* [WOODSTOCK, VT.: JEWISH LIGHTS PUBLISHING, 1995], PP. 99, 107)

Suggestions for Parenting Siblings

By Dr. Alan J. Levin

- While it is not possible to avoid comparing children when thinking about behaviors and developmental milestones, control the temptation to compare children in family conversation or when disciplining.

- We want to be fair to our children, but they are individuals and they may have different needs. For example, some children know that you love them with a kiss good night or because you play ball with them. Another child may look to you for constant affirmation, with words and kisses, that he or she is loved. Be sensitive to those individual needs.

- We like our rules to be consistent for family members, but it is sometimes appropriate to have different rules for children in the same family. For example, you may not have created a curfew for a child who was always home in the evening very early. Her brother may stay out late, resulting in the need for a curfew. That same child may then complain that his sister never had a curfew. Make the best decision at that time, provide a simple explanation, and then do not feel guilt. It is not possible to treat the two children exactly the same.

- Avoid stereotypes of children based on gender or birth order. Age or gender does not equal responsibility, sensitivity, or entitlement.

Alan J. Levin, Ph.D., is regional educator for the Great Lakes Council/Chicago Federation of the Union for Reform Judaism and project director of *CHAI: Learning for Jewish Life.*

Torah Session 3
Parenting Jewish Children (For Parents Who Are Non-Jews, Jewish by Choice, or Jewish by Birth)

Introduction

As Reform Jews, we strive to include all of our families in both synagogue life and Jewish life, regardless of background. It is also the task of our congregations to continue reaching out and assisting our families in their Jewish journeys. This session seeks to open dialogue and conversation on issues that directly affect our interfaith families. By addressing feelings of otherness, we acknowledge the sometimes difficult life journeys that our members face, while providing them tools for coping with these issues. It is important to state from the outset that this session is not about conversion or a first step toward conversion. Additionally, couples in which both partners are Jewish will also benefit from participation in this session, both by becoming more aware of their own Jewish connections and by learning more about the issues facing interfaith families. Other possible outcomes that your congregation may want to encourage could include:

- A continuation of the dialogue about these topics between participants and their spouses or partners after the session ends.
- Conversations between the participants and the rabbi or other Jewish professional (for example, Union for Reform Judaism outreach personnel, either on the regional or national level) regarding questions and/or concerns about interfaith issues.
- Enrollment of participants in an Introduction to Judaism course or other informational course on Judaism.
- The creation of an ongoing dialogue and friendship group to continue to explore these issues.

Enduring Understanding

Nurturing a strong Jewish identity requires the active participation of parents in their children's Jewish living and learning experiences.

Essential Questions

1. Who am I as a Jewish parent and a Jewish role model?
2. How does one establish a sacred relationship between parent and child?

3. What makes a meaningful Jewish life?

4. What does it mean to be a Jewish family?

Questions to Be Addressed

1. What does it mean for me to raise Jewish children?

2. What resources are available to help me raise Jewish children?

Evidence of Understanding

- Participants will engage in dialogue and problem solving about the challenges of raising Jewish children.
- Participants will complete the Jewish Learning Action Plan.

Session Overview

- Set Induction (30–40 minutes)
- Text Study and Discussion (40 minutes)
- Conclusion (30 minutes)

Materials Needed

- Paper, pens, or pencils
- Photocopies of the handout materials (pages 23–28)
- Chalkboard and chalk or flip chart and markers

SESSION PLAN

Set Induction (30–40 minutes)

The purpose of this activity is to build a bond of community within the group.

1. Create discussion groups of no more than eight participants each. Distribute paper and pencils or pens to each participant. Direct them to divide the sheet of paper in half, vertically, labeling the left side "Who I Am" and the right side "Issues." In the "Who I Am" column, ask participants to write descriptive words and brief sentences describing who they are. In the "Issues" column, ask participants to write issues that have emerged for them as parents who are raising Jewish children.

2. When they finish writing, ask the participants to share responses on their "Who I Am" list. Then ask the participants to share as much of the "Issues" side of the list as they feel comfortable. Allow time for discussion as participants share their responses.

Text Study and Discussion (40 minutes)

1. Distribute copies of the handouts on pages 23–28 and ask participants to turn to The Responsibilities of a Parent to a Child (page 27).

   Ask a volunteer to read the text aloud. Explain the following terms and concepts:

   - Circumcise (in Hebrew, *b'rit milah*)—This Jewish rite is exclusively for male children. *B'rit milah* is not simply a surgical procedure, but creates a physical mark of one's Jewish identity and signifies that a boy has entered into the Jewish covenant. Girls enter the covenant when they are given a Hebrew name.

   - Redeem (in Hebrew, *pidyon haben*)—A ceremony held on the thirty-first day after birth, this ritual releases the first-born male child from certain traditional responsibilities. While this ceremony is still observed in some communities, it is not usually observed by Reform Jews.

   - Teach a child Torah—Parents are partners in the religious education of their children. Some would say that parents are the primary Jewish educators of their children.

   - Children and marriage—In ancient times, parents arranged for the marriages of their children. Rabbi David Hartman explains that in contemporary times this means parents are to establish a home and family structure that creates in the child the capacity to love and function in a marriage or partnership.[1]

   - Teach a child a craft—This allows for the child to become economically self-sufficient.

   - Teach a child how to swim—Simply put, parents are to teach this physical survival skill to their children. In *Joy and Responsibility: Israel, Modernity and the Renewal of Judaism*, Rabbi Hartman expands the notion of what this means. He explains that a parent is to teach the child how to cope with life's unpredictable circumstances and events, and how to handle crises and emergencies and everyday challenges.[2]

2. Invite the group to discuss the following questions. Write their answers to the second question on the board or flip chart.

   - In your opinion, are these responsibilities still relevant today? Are there any others you would add? *(Observing Shabbat and Jewish holidays, teaching children about giving* tzedakah, *creating a Jewish home environment, etc.)*

   - Given the responsibilities we have identified for raising Jewish children, what are the greatest challenges you face as the parent of a Jewish child?

---

[1]David Hartman, *Joy and Responsibility: Israel, Modernity, and the Renewal of Judaism* (Jerusalem: Ben-Zvi Publishers, 1978), p. 87.
[2]Ibid.

3. Select three or four of the challenges the group has identified and divide the participants into the same number of teams. Assign each team one of the challenges and ask the participants to come up with a few strategies that could be employed for addressing that challenge. (For example, if an identified challenge is lack of parental Jewish knowledge, then a strategy for addressing it might be enrollment in an adult education class at the synagogue.)

4. Bring the whole group back together and ask each team to share the strategies it identified for helping raise a Jewish child.

Conclusion (30 minutes)

1. Ask the participants to respond to this question:

   What have you learned today that you would like to apply to your own life and your own parenting?

2. Ask the participants to look at the Web resources on page 23. If facilities allow, set up a computer with Internet access so that the participants can view the suggested Web sites. If possible, also make available a library resource of books and materials from the suggested bibliography on interfaith relationships, basic Judaism, and conversion. Invite the session participants to "browse and borrow" from this collection. (You may also want to hand out additional information about classes and other learning opportunities available through your synagogue.)

3. If time permits, ask the participants to complete the Jewish Learning Action Plan found on page 28. If there is no time left to do this, ask them to complete the Plan at home and to post it in a prominent place, both as a reminder to themselves and also as a model for their children, indicating their commitment to lifelong Jewish learning.

Resources

Web sites

www.urj.org/outreach/	Union for Reform Judaism Department of Outreach and Synagogue Community
www.clickonjudaism.org/	clickonJudaism webzine
www.interfaithfamily.com/	InterfaithFamily.com
www.joi.com/	Jewish Outreach Institute
www.urj.org/educate/parent/	The Jewish Parent Page

Bibliography

Suggested by the URJ Department of Outreach and Synagogue Community

Conversion/Choosing Judaism

Berkowitz, Rabbi Allan L., and Patti Moskovitz. *Embracing the Covenant.* Woodstock, Vt.: Jewish Lights Publishing, 1996.
Diamant, Anita. *Choosing a Jewish Life.* New York: Schocken Books, Inc., 1998.
Epstein, Lawrence J. *Questions and Answers on Conversion to Judaism.* Northvale, N.J.: Jason Aronson, Inc., 1998.
Epstein, Lawrence J. *Readings on Conversion to Judaism.* Northvale, N.J.: Jason Aronson, Inc., 1995.
Homolka, Walter, Walter Jacob, and Esther Seidel. *Not By Birth Alone: Conversion to Judaism.* London: Cassell, 1997.
Kessel, Barbara. *Suddenly Jewish.* Lebanon, N.H.: University Press of New England, 2000.
Kling, Simcha, revised by Carl M. Perkins. *Embracing Judaism.* New York: The Rabbinical Assembly, 1999.
Kukoff, Lydia. *Choosing Judaism.* New York: UAHC Press, 1981.
Lester, Julius. *Lovesong: Becoming a Jew.* New York: Henry Holt & Company, 1995.
McClain, Ellen Jaffe. *Embracing the Stranger.* New York: Basic Books, Inc., 1995.
Myrowitz, Catherine Hall. *Finding a Home for the Soul.* Northvale, N.J.: Jason Aronson, Inc., 1995.

Interfaith Relationships

Cowan, Paul, with Rachel Cowan. *Mixed Blessings: Overcoming the Stumbling Blocks in an Interfaith Marriage.* New York: Penguin Books, Inc., 1989.

Friedland, Ronnie, and Edmund Case, editors. *The Guide to Jewish Interfaith Family Life: An InterfaithFamily.com Handbook.* Woodstock, Vt.: Jewish Lights Publishing, 2001.

Glaser, Gabrielle. *Strangers to the Tribe.* New York: Houghton Mifflin Co., 1997.

Hyman, Meryl. *Who Is a Jew?* Woodstock, Vt.: Jewish Lights Publishing, 1998.

King, Andrea. *If I'm Jewish and You're Christian, What Are the Kids?* New York: UAHC Press, 1993.

Petsonk, Judy, and Jim Remsen. *The Intermarriage Handbook: A Guide for Jews and Christians.* New York: HarperCollins Publishers, 1991.

Schneider, Susan Weidman. *Intermarriage: The Challenge of Living With Differences Between Christians and Jews.* New York: Simon and Schuster, 1990.

Introduction to Judaism and Jewish Living

Catalano, Rosann, David Sandmel, and Christopher Leighton, eds. *Irreconcilable Differences? A Learning Resource for Jews and Christians.* Boulder, Co.: Westview Press, 2001.

Cohen, Henry. *What's Special about Judaism?* Philadelphia: XLibris, 2002.

Diamant, Anita, and Howard Cooper. *Living a Jewish Life.* New York: HarperPerennial, 1996.

Einstein, Stephen J., and Lydia Kukoff. *Every Person's Guide to Judaism.* New York: UAHC Press, 1989.

Hertzberg, Arthur, and Aron Hirt-Manheimer. *Jews: The Essences and Character of a People.* San Francisco: HarperSanFrancisco, 1998.

Kertzer, Morris. Revised by Rabbi Lawrence Hoffman. *What Is a Jew?* New York: Collier Books, 1997.

Knobel, Peter, ed. *Gates of the Season: A Guide to the Jewish Year.* New York: CCAR Press, 1992.

Kushner, Harold. *To Life! A Celebration of Jewish Being and Thinking.* New York: Little, Brown, & Co., 1994.

Maslin, Simeon, ed. *Gates of Mitzvah: A Guide to the Jewish Life Cycle.* New York: CCAR Press, 1979.

Perelson, Ruth. *Invitation to Shabbat.* New York: UAHC Press, 1997.

Schulman, Zell. *Let My People Eat! Passover Seders Made Simple.* New York: Hungry Minds, Inc., 1998.

Shapiro, Mark Dov. *Gates of Shabbat: A Guide for Observing Shabbat.* New York: CCAR Press, 1991.

Sonsino, Rifat, and Daniel B. Syme. *Finding God: Selected Responses* (rev. ed). New York: UAHC Press, 2002.

Steinberg, Milton. *Basic Judaism.* Orlando: Harcourt Brace Jovanovich, Inc., 1986.

Syme, Daniel B. *The Jewish Home: A Guide for Jewish Living.* New York: UAHC Press, 2004.

Telushkin, Joseph. *Jewish Literacy.* New York: William Morrow & Co. Inc., 1991.

Washofsky, Mark. *Jewish Living: A Guide to Contemporary Reform Practice.* New York: UAHC Press, 2001.

Zerin, Edward. *How to Explain Judaism to Your Non-Jewish Neighbor.* Los Angeles: Isaac Nathan Publishing Co., Inc., 1997.

Jewish Parenting

Abraham, Michelle Shapiro. *Good Morning, Boker Tov* and *Good Night, Lilah Tov.* New York: UAHC Press, 2002.

Abramowitz, Yosef I., and Susan Silverman. *Jewish Family and Life: Traditions, Holidays and Values for Today's Parents and Children.* New York: Golden Books, 1997.

Brichto, Mira Pollack. *The God Around Us: Unending Wonder.* New York: UAHC Press, 2001.

Danan, Julie Hilton. *The Jewish Parents' Almanac.* Northvale, N.J.: Jason Aronson, Inc., 1997.

Diamant, Anita. *The New Jewish Baby Book.* Woodstock, Vt.: Jewish Lights Publishing, 1994.

Freedman, B., Jan Greenberg, and Karen Katz. *What Does Being Jewish Mean? Read-Aloud Responses to Questions Jewish Children Ask About History, Culture and Religion.* New York: Prentice-Hall, Inc., 1991.

Gellman, Marc, and Thomas Hartman. *How Do You Spell God?* New York: William Morrow & Co., 1995.

Grishaver, Joel Lurie. *Ten Attitudes of Highly Effective Jewish Grandparents: Patterns for Enhancing & Sustaining Your Grandchildren's Jewishness.* Los Angeles: Torah Aura Productions, 1995.

Kurshan, Neil. *Raising Your Child to Be a Mensch.* New York: Simon and Schuster, 1987.

Kushner, Harold. *When Children Ask About God.* New York: Schocken Books, Inc., 1995.

Kushner, Lawrence, and Karen Kushner. *Because Nothing Looks Like God.* Woodstock, Vt.: Jewish Lights Publishing, 2001.

Mogel, Wendy. *The Blessing of a Skinned Knee: Using Jewish Teachings to Raise Self-Reliant Children.* New York: Penguin, 2001.
Olitzky, Kerry M., Steven M. Rosman, and David P. Kasakove. *When Your Jewish Child Asks Why: Answers for Tough Questions.* Hoboken, N.J.: KTAV Publishing House, Inc., 1993.
Sasso, Sandy. *God's Paintbrush.* Woodstock, Vt.: Jewish Lights Publishing, 1992.
Wolpe, David. *Teaching Your Children About God: A Modern Jewish Approach.* New York: Henry Holt & Co., 1995.

The Responsibilities of a Parent to a Child

The sages taught: A parent is obligated to do the following for his child: to circumcise, to redeem, to teach the child Torah, to teach the child a craft, and to get the child married. Some say, also to teach the child to swim. Rabbi Judah said: When a parent does not teach a child a craft, it is as though he taught him or her thievery. Rabbi Judah I, the Patriarch said: A parent is also required to teach the child civic obligations.

(BABYLONIAN TALMUD, *KIDDUSHIN* 29A)

Jewish Learning Action Plan

List the things you are already doing and will continue to do to raise your Jewish child (for example, sending my child to Religious School, celebrating Jewish holidays, etc.).

____

____

____

____

Things I can start doing soon and when I will start:

____

____

____

____

Things I plan to do in the future and when I will start:

____

____

____

____

*(Possible items include: Take adult education classes, learn Hebrew, buy/read resource books, find out more about holiday observances, enroll in 10 Minutes of Torah [**www.urj.org/torah/ten**] weekly online study, meet with rabbi, cantor, educator, start a Jewish study or book club, etc.)*

Torah Session 4
V'higaditah L'vanecha: And You Shall Tell Your Child on That Day

Introduction

This session provides participants a forum in which to study the holiday of Passover, specifically through the vehicle of the Haggadah. It also includes a guided activity for reviewing and selecting Haggadot that will be most appropriate and useful for the participants and their families. The session ends with the parents receiving a resource handbook for the celebration of Passover, created especially for *CHAI: Parent Education*—a benefit of attendance that you may want to feature in any publicity about this session. Please note that for this session, participants should be asked beforehand to bring with them a copy of the Haggadah they may already be using. In addition, a display of many different Haggadot for the participants to review will need to be available. Sources for Haggadot include the temple library, the rabbi, the educator, the temple gift shop, local Jewish bookstores, or online retailers. If funds for purchasing Haggadot are not available, the sponsoring group or the congregation may need to consider charging a fee to cover those costs. An added benefit of purchasing these Haggadot is the creation of a permanent resource for the congregation.

It should be noted that non-Jewish parents who are raising Jewish children or parents who are Jews-by-Choice may be among the participants in your group. Since these participants will most likely not have the kind of memories of Passover seders that others in the group may have, it is important to treat this topic with sensitivity and care.

Enduring Understanding

Nurturing a strong Jewish identity requires the active participation of parents in their children's Jewish living and learning experiences.

Essential Questions

1. Who am I as a Jewish parent and a Jewish role model?
2. How does one establish a sacred relationship between parent and child?
3. What makes a meaningful Jewish life?
4. What does it mean to be a Jewish family?

Questions to Be Addressed

1. What does Passover mean to me? To my family? To the Jewish people?
2. What Jewish historical experience do we recreate with the seder?
3. How can I create meaningful Passover experiences for my family?
4. In what ways does the Haggadah affect the Passover experience for my family?
5. What are the connections between the history, the ceremonial foods, the prayers, and the songs of the Passover seder?

Evidence of Understanding

- Participants will be able to retell the story of the Exodus from Egypt and why we still celebrate that event today.
- Participants will reflect on their own Passover memories and family traditions, and discuss the experiences and memories they hope to create for their child(ren).
- Participants will make an informed choice of a Haggadah that will be meaningful for their family and that will enhance their celebration of Passover.

Session Overview

- Set Induction (10 minutes)
- Text Study: *Parashat Bo* (20–25 minutes)
- Group Learning: Haggadah Overview (15–20 minutes)
- Choosing a Haggadah (20–25 minutes)
- Group Sharing (10 minutes)
- Conclusion (5 minutes)

Materials Needed

- Variety of Haggadot collected and organized by the presenter
- Chalkboard and chalk or flip chart and markers
- Photocopies of handouts (pages 33–36)
- Photocopies of *V'higaditah L'vanecha:* And You Shall Tell Your Child on That Day, a resource handbook on Passover, for each participant (pages 37–47).

SESSION PLAN

Set Induction (10 minutes)

Ask the participants to reminisce about their Passover experiences. Share with them that whether these experiences are recent or from childhood, whether they are born Jews or new to Judaism, all of them have experiences to share. These experiences become their Passover memories.

Ask the group:

- What are your Passover memories? (If you did not celebrate Passover as a child, what are your impressions of the holiday, based on anything you may have experienced or heard about it?)
- Who led the seder?
- Which Haggadah was used?
- Who cooked? What was cooked?
- Who was invited? Did you sing songs?
- Did your family complete the seder?
- What traditions and observances made/make Passover special for you?
- How did your observance fulfill the biblical commandment to "observe this [Passover] as an institution for all time, for you and for your descendants" (Exodus 12:24)?

Text study: *Parashat Bo* (20–25 minutes)

1. Distribute copies of the handouts on pages 33–36.
2. Ask for volunteers to read the texts on page 33 aloud as the participants follow along.
3. Ask the group to discuss the following questions:
    - What are we being commanded to do in these verses?
    - What did *Adonai* do for us and our ancestors?
    - What is the phrase in these texts that commands us to relive the Exodus as if it happened to us?
    - Describe how the seder recreates the Exodus experience.
    - How does eating matzah help recreate our ancestors' experience?
    - What does God expect of parents in these verses?

Group Learning: Haggadah Overview (15–20 minutes)

1. Share with the participants that Haggadah is a Hebrew word that means "telling" or "explanation." In the book of Exodus we read, "And you shall tell your child on that day, 'It is because of what *Adonai*

did for me when I went free from Egypt'" (Exodus 13:8). We are commanded to experience Passover as if the Exodus were our own experience. We are to feel that we were slaves in Egypt and that we gained our freedom during the Exodus. We relive the Exodus experience by participating in a Passover seder.

2. Review with participants The Seder in 15 Steps on page 35.

Choosing a Haggadah (20–25 minutes)

1. Explain to participants that a crucial step in creating a successful Passover seder is choosing a Haggadah (pl. Haggadot) that works for one's family. Ask the participants to relate any experiences with Haggadot they may have used:
   - What did you like about the Haggadah?
   - What could have been better or different?
   - What would you like to see in a Haggadah?
   - What elements would make it more meaningful for you and your family?
2. Choose one Haggadah and go through the Haggadah Review Question Sheet (page 36) with the participants, demonstrating what their task will be when they are reviewing a Haggadah.
3. Ask each participant to browse the Haggadah display, choosing one Haggadah to examine. The participants may also opt to review their own Haggadah. Provide additional copies of the Haggadah Review Question sheet for each Haggadah that a participant will review. The participants will use the questions provided to review the Haggadah that they chose. Time and resources permitting, ask the participants to review additional Haggadot.

Group Sharing (10 minutes)

1. Reassemble the group. Ask each participant to share his/her thoughts and reactions to the Haggadot he/she reviewed. Record responses on the chalkboard or poster under the title of each Haggadah (pre-written on chalkboard or flip chart) as participants give their answers. Also ask: What is the Haggadah trying to teach? Did you think the Haggadah was "user/family friendly"?
2. Invite the participants to examine the Haggadot reviewed by the other participants, choosing those that appeal to them. The reviews by the other participants should help them in choosing which additional Haggadot they wish to examine. Be sure to inform the participants how to locate and purchase the Haggadot that are displayed.

Conclusion (5 minutes)

1. Ask participants to share with the group any important new learning about Passover or to show which of the Haggadot they choose to use at their own seders.
2. Distribute copies of *V'higaditah L'vanecha*—And You Shall Tell Your Child on That Day (pages 37–47).

Text Study: *Parashat Bo*

This day shall be to you one of remembrance: you shall celebrate it as a festival to Adonai *throughout the ages; you shall celebrate it as an institution for all time. Seven days you shall eat unleavened bread.*
(EXODUS 12:14–15)

*You shall observe the [Feast of] Unleavened Bread, for on this very day I [*Adonai*] brought your ranks out of the land of Egypt; you shall observe this day throughout the ages as an institution for all time. In the first month, from the fourteenth day of the month at evening, you shall eat unleavened bread until the twenty-first day of the month at evening.*
(EXODUS 12:17–18)

You shall observe this as an institution for all time, for you and for your descendants. And when you enter the land that Adonai *will give you, as God has promised, you shall observe this rite. And when your children ask you, "What do you mean by this rite?" You shall say, "It is the passover sacrifice to* Adonai, *because God passed over the houses of the Israelites in Egypt when God smote the Egyptians, but saved our houses."*
(EXODUS 12:24–27)

And they baked unleavened cakes of the dough that they had taken out of Egypt, for it was not leavened, since they had been driven out of Egypt and could not delay; nor had they prepared any provisions for themselves. The length of time that the Israelites lived in Egypt was four hundred and thirty years; at the end of the four hundred and thirtieth year, to the very day, all the ranks of Adonai *departed from the land of Egypt. That was for* Adonai *a night of vigil to bring them out of the land of Egypt; that same night is* Adonai*'s, one of vigil for all the children of Israel throughout the ages.*
(EXODUS 12:39–42)

Discussion Questions

1. What are we being commanded to do in these verses?
2. What did *Adonai* do for us and our ancestors?
3. What is the phrase in these texts that commands us to relive the Exodus as if it happened to us?
4. Describe how the seder recreates the Exodus experience.
5. How does eating matzah help recreate our ancestors' experience?
6. What does God expect of parents in these verses?

The Seder in 15 Steps or The Essential Haggadah

קַדֵּשׁ	*Kadeish*—Sanctifying the day (blessing over the first cup of wine)
וּרְחַץ	*Ur'chatz*—Washing the hands (may or may not be included in liberal Haggadot)
כַּרְפַּס	*Karpas*—Blessing over the greens
יַחַץ	*Yachatz*—Breaking the middle matzah, creating the *afikoman*
מַגִּיד	*Magid*—Telling the story of Passover
רָחְצָה	*Rochtza*—Washing the hands (may or may not be included in liberal Haggadot)
מוֹצִיא	*Motzi*—Blessing over the bread, which for Passover is the matzah
מַצָּה	Matzah—Blessing specifically over the matzah
מָרוֹר	*Maror*—Blessing over the bitter herbs
כּוֹרֵךְ	*Koreich*—Eating the Hillel sandwich
שֻׁלְחָן עוֹרֵךְ	*Shulchan Oreich*—Dinner
צָפוּן	*Tzafun*—Eating the *afikoman*
בָּרֵךְ	*Bareich*—*Birkat HaMazon* (blessing after eating)
הַלֵּל	*Hallel*—Songs of praise
נִרְצָה	*Nirtzah*—Conclusion of the seder: Next year in Jerusalem!

Haggadah Review Question Sheet

Title of the Haggadah: ______________________________

Author/Publisher of the Haggadah: ______________________________

If your children are readers, could they follow along and read from this Haggadah?

____

Do you like and understand the English readings? Are they meaningful to you?

____

Does the Haggadah include transliterations of the Hebrew prayers and blessings? Is this important to you? ______________________________

Does the Haggadah include complete instructions for organizing a seder and for the seven-day (eight days if it is a traditional Haggadah) Passover observance?

____

Are these instructions necessary for your family or will you be able to locate additional sources if necessary? ______________________________

What part does artwork play in the Haggadah? Does it appeal to you? Would it appeal to your family? ______________________________

Does this Haggadah look like it would fit or suit your family's needs at this time?

____

Does the Haggadah engage you? Is it one that your family would enjoy using from year to year? ______________________________

V'higaditah L'vanecha—And You Shall Tell Your Child on That Day

Contents

Vocabulary

seder סֵדֶר (pl. **s'darim** סְדָרִים)—This Hebrew word means "order." We call our Passover meal a seder because of the order of prayers, readings, and explanations contained in the Haggadah that we use to retell the story of Passover every year. The Passover seder is held on the first night of the holiday in Israel and in many Reform households. A seder is traditionally held on the second night outside the Land of Israel and by Conservative and Orthodox Jews. Many Reform Jews choose to observe a second night seder. The seder we know today developed over hundreds of years, but the basic rules and order we follow were described in the Mishnah:

> *Rabban Gamaliel used to say: Whoever does not make mention of the following three things on Passover does not fulfill the mitzvot of observing Passover: the Passover-offering, the unleavened bread, and the bitter herbs. The Passover offering (the sacrifice made in honor of the holiday), done because* Adonai *passed over the houses of our ancestors in Egypt, as it says in the Torah,*

"It is the passover sacrifice to Adonai, *because* Adonai *passed over the houses of the Israelites in Egypt when Adonai smote the Egyptians, but saved our houses" (Exodus 12:27).*

The unleavened bread (matzah) is eaten because our ancestors were redeemed from Egypt. This teaching is based on the verse: "And they baked unleavened cakes of the dough that they had taken out of Egypt, for it was not leavened, since they had been driven out of Egypt and could not delay; nor had they prepared any provisions for themselves" (Exodus 12:39).

The bitter herbs are eaten because the Egyptians embittered the lives of our ancestors in Egypt, for it says in the Torah, "The Egyptians ruthlessly imposed upon the Israelites the various labors that they made them perform. Ruthlessly they made life bitter for them with harsh labor at mortar and bricks and with all sorts of tasks in the field" (Exodus 1:13–14).

Rabban Gamliel also taught: In every generation each of us is bound to regard him/herself as though he/she had personally gone forth from Egypt, because it says in the Torah, "And you shall tell your child on that day, saying: It is because of that which Adonai *did for me when I came forth out of Egypt" (Exodus 13:8).*

(*P'SACHIM* 10:5)

matzah מַצָּה (pl. **matzot** מַצּוֹת)—The unleavened bread we eat during Passover. In the Book of Deuteronomy we are reminded, "You shall not eat anything leavened with it [the Passover sacrifice]; for seven days thereafter you shall eat unleavened bread, bread of affliction, for you departed from the land of Egypt hurriedly, so that you may remember the day of your departure from the land of Egypt as long as you live" (Deuteronomy 16:3).

Three symbolic matzot are placed on the seder table, each of which is placed separately in the folds of a napkin or in a special matzah cover, which has three pockets. There are several interpretations of these three symbolic matzot. One says that the top and bottom matzot correspond to the two challot that are traditional on Shabbat. The third matzah is specifically for Passover and becomes our *afikoman.* Another interpretation is that the three matzot represent the three categories of the Jewish people: Kohanim, Levi'im, and Israelites.

Additional matzot are also placed on the seder table for consumption during the seder.

afikoman אֲפִיקוֹמָן—The middle matzah of the two symbolic matzot. *Afikoman,* a Greek word, means dessert. Traditionally this is the last item eaten on seder night. There are two other traditions associated with the *afikoman.* One is that after the middle matzah is broken and wrapped, the seder leader sets it aside and the children at the seder steal it. The second tradition is that the seder leader wraps the broken middle matzah in a napkin, hides it, and the children must then search for it. In either case the *afikoman* is ransomed back by the seder leader so that the seder may conclude.

The seder plate contains the following symbolic foods:

maror מָרוֹר	The bitter vegetable, usually horseradish, symbolizing the bitterness of slavery. On some seder plates there is also a space for another bitter tasting vegetable called *hasaf,* meaning lettuce in Hebrew. Often romaine lettuce, which has a bitter taste, is used.
beitzah בֵּיצָה	A roasted egg, symbol of the continuing cycle of life and the extra festival sacrifice given in the days of the Temple in Jerusalem to honor the holiday of Passover.
karpas כַּרְפַּס	A green vegetable such as parsley, lettuce, or celery. A symbol of spring and the rebirth of the earth.
z'roa זְרוֹעַ	The roasted shankbone, which reminds us of the first Passover sacrifice (Exodus 12:3–10) and later the Passover sacrifice offering brought to the Temple in Jerusalem.
charoset חֲרֹסֶת	A combination of fruits and nuts with wine or grape juice. *Charoset* is not mentioned in the Torah as part of the observances of Passover. How *charoset* came about is unclear, but the Rabbis of the Talmud discussed a variety of reasons why *charoset* was an important part of the Passover seder experience:

> ***Rabbi Eleazar son of Rabbi Zadok said: The charoset is a religious requirement. Why is it a religious requirement? he asked. Rabbi Levi said: In memory of the apple tree [the place where Israelite women were said to give birth]; Rabbi Yohanan said: In memory of the clay [which the Israelites baked into bricks]. Abaye observed: Therefore one must make it acrid and thicken it, in memory of the clay. It was taught in accordance with Rabbi Yohanan: The spices are in memory of the straw [in those days cinnamon and ginger could not be ground well and contained some threads which looked like the straw the Israelites kneaded into the clay] and so the charoset itself is a reminder of the clay.***
>
> (*P'SACHIM* 115–116A)

Organizing Your Seder

For those who have never put a seder together it may seem like an overwhelming task. But with some organization it can be done!

- Have your family help. Create a list of assignments or a Passover task chart and delegate the duties, filling in the names of family and friends who have volunteered for jobs. Even the youngest of your children will be able to contribute. Sharing the preparations for Passover makes it more meaningful for everyone. Tasks may include: cleaning, meal planning, shopping, cooking, writing special readings to include at the seder, setting the table, making place cards, creating a centerpiece, and preparing individual seder plates with the ritual foods.
- Decide in advance who will lead the seder. The duties of the seder leader should include reading over the Haggadah before the seder, deciding what is to be read in Hebrew and what in English, what parts might be skipped, and where discussion questions, innovations, and family traditions can be added in.
- Plan the menu and choose items that can be made in advance. Share the food preparations with your seder guests. Ask your guests if there are special foods they would like to prepare for the seder. Consider putting together a Passover recipe book to give to all your guests. Visit your local grocery stores and Jewish/kosher markets. There are many products available that will make seder tasks easier.
- Make sure that each seder participant has a Haggadah. The seder will run more smoothly if all the seder participants have the same Haggadah.
- Encourage participation by rotating the readings from the Haggadah among the guests.
- Sing the holiday songs. There are many tapes and CDs available with Passover music to help you learn the melodies. (See page 46.)

Innovations for Your Passover Seder

- All Jewish celebrations include opportunities for *tzedakah*—sharing with the less fortunate. In the Mishnah, it is taught that even the poorest person must recline at the seder and have four cups of wine, even if this poor person is supported by community charity (*P'sachim* 10:1). There are many ways to include *tzedakah* in your celebration of Passover. Two ways to help are by giving a donation to the community fund for Passover, called *"Maot Hittin"* in Hebrew, or make a donation to your synagogue earmarked for Passover funds for the needy. If you are clearing out *chameitz* (products that contain leavening) from your home, you can donate unopened packages of leavened products to a local food bank

- There is a custom among Sephardic Jews of putting a piece of matzah in a bag, placing it over the shoulder of one of the seder participants and having that person walk around the seder table, physically re-enacting the Exodus from Egypt. After breaking the middle matzah, creating the *afikoman,* wrap it in a napkin or small bag and invite all the seder participants to take a freedom walk around the table or around the house.

- "Dayenu" is a traditional Passover song of praise to *Adonai* for all the miracles that led to our freedom. Ask the seder participants to add another *dayenu*/miracle/special event or occurrence that happened since last Passover and for which they are especially thankful.

- Jews have always been influenced by the cuisine of the many different countries in which they have lived. In addition to the three recipes included here, collect a variety of charoset recipes from cookbooks, friends, relatives, and the Internet and choose two or more to make for your seder this year. This might be a great research opportunity for a child.

Ashkenazi Charoset

Ingredients:
3 apples, red, green, or yellow (peeled if desired)
1 cup chopped walnuts or almonds
½ tsp. of cinnamon
1–3 tbsp. sweet red wine or grape juice
honey or sugar to taste (optional)

Preparation:
Chop and blend the ingredients.

Yemenite Charoset

Ingredients:
30 dates
20 figs
4 tbsp. sesame seeds
2 tsp. ginger powder

matzah meal, as desired
dry red wine
1 chili pepper (optional)

Preparation:
Use a food processor to mix all ingredients into a paste.

Middle Eastern Charoset

2 oz. pine nuts
2 hard boiled egg yolks
1 apple, grated
3 oz. ground almonds
juice and rind of 1 lemon
cinnamon and allspice, to taste
3 oz. raisins
$\frac{1}{3}$ c. sugar

Mix all ingredients, adjust sugar and spices to taste.

- Passover is not only a time of learning about our people's history on a grand scale, but can also be an opportunity to learn about our own history on a smaller scale. During the seder dinner ask the seder participants to retell the historical events of their families. This could include stories of immigration, survival, adjustment to a new land, learning a new language, or love stories.

- Traditionally the ransom for the *afikoman* was money. As with many of the seder activities this was also meant to capture the attention of children. Many parents would like something other than a monetary payment for the finder of the *afikoman.* Consider some of the following: a story, a song, a donation to a favorite charity in the name of the child holding the *afikoman,* a donation in honor of all the children at the seder, or a tangible gift like a storybook with a Jewish theme, or a Hebrew or Jewish CD or game.

- Miriam's Cup *(Kos Miryam)* is a relatively new tradition in which we place a special cup on the seder table to honor of Miriam, sister of Moses. Miriam played a vital role in the history of our people; it is said that due to her merit a well of water followed the Israelites during their forty-year wandering through the desert. Miriam's Cup is a special goblet filled with water and placed on the seder table. Before reciting the ritual related to the cup of Elijah, we celebrate Miriam's Cup.

A Suggested Ritual for Miriam's Cup *(Kos Miryam)*

Have a water-filled goblet on the table, or if each seder participant has a water glass, each one can pour some water from his or her own cup to fill the *Kos Miryam.*

Raise Miriam's Cup and recite together:

Miriam, a prophetess, predicted the birth of her baby brother Moses, guarded him as he floated down the Nile, witnessed Pharaoh's daughter drawing him out of the river, and arranged for their own mother to care for the infant Moses. Miriam was over eighty when she kicked up her heels and led the women in joyous dancing, celebrating the Israelites' safe crossing through the Sea of Reeds and their escape from slavery in Egypt. A symbol of her special place in the life of the Jewish people was the miraculous well known as Miriam's Well that quenched the thirst of our people during their forty-year trek in the desert. We place on our seder table this special Cup of Miriam to remember this remarkable woman who was a prophetess, dancer, and guardian of our people.

- At the close of your seder, create a circle of sharing by asking each seder participant to share something he or she learned about Passover this year or what he or she liked best about the seder.

Family Craft Activities

Matzah Cover

Use four squares of fabric or finished handkerchiefs large enough to cover a board of matzah, with an additional inch of fabric for the seam allowance (12" squares will work well). Decorate the top-most fabric square with fabric paints, crayons, or appliqué of additional fabric. If you choose to appliqué designs of cut-out fabric on to the fabric square, it may be either sewn on or adhered with an adhesive fabric bond. One such product is called Heat and Bond. Craft and fabric stores will be able to assist you. Next, layer the four pieces of fabric together, with the decorated square uppermost. Sew the four pieces together on three sides, leaving the fourth side open, allowing you to insert the matzah.

Afikoman Cover

Fold a square of fabric 12" x 18" into thirds and press. Open up one third and sew the remaining folded fabric on the two short sides, creating a pouch. Decorate the outside of the upper third with fabric paints, crayons, or appliqué.

Paint-It-Yourself Ritual Items

In many communities there are paint-it-yourself ceramic shops. There may be aspiring artists in your family who would enjoy making one or more of the Passover ritual items for the family (seder plate, *Kos Eliyahu*/Cup of Elijah, *kiddush* cups, candlesticks, matzah plate, etc.). Consider taking a family field trip and having each family member make a different item for the Passover table.

Reclining on Pillows

It is a tradition that we are to recline at the Passover seder. This symbolizes that we are free. We recline by placing pillows on the chairs of the seder participants so they may lean against them. With your family, create decorated pillowcases as covers for the pillows that will be used during the seder. Use fabric paints on freshly laundered pillowcases, and follow manufacturers' directions for the paints. Fabric paints are available in most craft stores. Consider using phrases from the Haggadah, Passover symbols, and/or simple designs to decorate the pillowcases.

A Few More Ideas

- Set up a Passover recipe-sharing group. The easiest way to do this may be via the Internet. Set up a listserv of individuals who would like to share recipes. This listserv may also become a forum for follow-up questions about the seder, Haggadah, or any other Passover issues. If the Internet is not feasible, use the temple bulletin to post recipes or communicate the old-fashioned way, through regular mail.

- If your congregation is far from shops that carry products for Passover, organize a carpool for shopping in the nearest large city that has stores with these products.

- In most small communities there are grocery stores that do carry some Passover products. Speak to the manager to learn what products will be carried, when they will arrive, and ask if it is possible to order specific items.

- Consider joining with other families to organize a group seder, sharing not only the preparations but also the making of Passover memories.

Preparing the House for Passover

There are many levels of observance when it comes to Passover food restrictions. Some Reform Jewish households remove all traces of *chameitz* (leavened products) from their homes for Passover and some families do not. Also, many families remove all leavened products but do not observe the full ritual for its removal, while some families do. The following is an explanation of *chameitz* and the three-step ritual for cleansing your home of leaven.

Chameitz—This word means "leaven." It is the term given to those foods that are traditionally forbidden during Passover. In their haste to leave Egypt, the Israelites only had time to bake unleavened bread—matzah. To remind us of the experience of the Exodus, we are commanded to eat matzah. The Rabbis extended this law and forbade any leavened products. *Chameitz* is any leavened product made from wheat, oats, barley, rye, or spelt. Ashkenazi (European) Jews later added rice, corn, peas, beans, and peanuts to the list. Jews who strictly observe Passover thoroughly clean their homes of all *chameitz* just before the holiday.

While many Reform Jewish homes do not participate in the following ceremony, it is a unique experience that may encourage your children to see the special qualities of Passover.

Bedikat Chameitz—The search for leaven is done the night before the first seder when all cleaning is finished. Traditionally the search is done with a candle, in order to see into the corners of the house, a feather for brushing up crumbs, and a wooden spoon to hold these crumbs. All of these items can be burned during the last part of the ritual. Before the search the following is recited:

בָּרוּךְ אַתָּה יְיָ אֱלֹהֵינוּ מֶלֶךְ הָעוֹלָם, אֲשֶׁר קִדְּשָׁנוּ בְּמִצְוֹתָיו, וְצִוָּנוּ
עַל בִּיעוּר חָמֵץ.

> *Baruch atah Adonai, Eloheinu Melech haolam, asher kid'shanu b'mitzvotav v'tzivanu al biur chameitz.*
>
> Praised are You, Eternal our God, Sovereign of the universe, who has sanctified us with commandments and commanded us to remove all *chameitz.*

Typically several small piles of crumbs are left around the home to be found by the searchers.

Bittul Chameitz—This is the formula of nullification regarding *chameitz*. It is recited after the search at night: "All leaven in my possession which I have not seen or removed or of which I am unaware is hereby nullified and ownerless as the dust of the earth."

Biur Chameitz—This is done on the morning after the search for leaven and takes place before 10:00 A.M. on the day of the seder. All the *chameitz* found along with the candle, spoon, and feather are burned. A barbeque grill is probably the safest place to do this and should always be done under adult supervision.

Family Discussion

- In the spirit of Reform Judaism, we make decisions regarding Jewish practices based on knowledge. Which of the practices regarding the ritual of removing *chameitz* from our home make sense for our family?
- Which Passover food customs would be meaningful for our family to observe? What about Passover kashrut and kashrut in general?

Bibliography

Abramowitz, Yosef, I., and Susan Silverman. *Jewish Family and Life Traditions, Holidays, and Values for Today's Parents and Children.* New York: Golden Books, 1997.

Danan, Julie Hilton. *The Jewish Parents' Almanac.* Northvale, N.J.: Jason Aronson, Inc., 1993.

Schwartz, Frances Weinman. *Passage to Pesach: Preparing for Passover Through Text and Tradition.* New York: UAHC Press, 2003.

Zion, Noam, and David Dishon. *A Different Night: The Family Participation Haggadah.* Jerusalem, Israel: The Shalom Hartman Institute, 1997.

Passover Cookbooks

(There are dozens. Here are just a few.)

Ashkanazi-Hankin, Gail. *Festivals of Lite Kosher Cookbook.* Gretna, La.: Pelican Publishing Co., 1999

AvRutick, Frances R. *The Complete Passover Cookbook.* New York: Jonathan David Publishers, 1981.

Nathan, Joan. *The Jewish Holiday Kitchen.* New York: Schocken Books, Inc., 1998.

Rauchwerger, Lisa. *Chocolate Chip Challah and Other Twists on the Jewish Holiday Table.* New York: UAHC Press, 1999.

Web Resources

Music for the seder

www.soundswrite.com (Soundswrite Productions)
www.transcontinentalmusic.com (Transcontinental Music Publications)

For Haggadot

www.amazon.com (Amazon.com)
www.BN.com (Barnes and Noble)

For Passover recipes

www.kosher4passover.com/recipes.htm

Torah Session 5
The Land of Israel: Exploring Our Connection, Connecting Our Children

The purpose of this session is to help participants understand the ongoing connection and attachment of the Jewish people to the Land of Israel over the ages as a framework within which they can define or search for their own connection. It is likely, however, that any discussion that touches upon the subject of Israel today may raise questions about the difficulties of the present political situation and Israel's problematic relationship with her neighbors. These questions, feelings, and reactions should, of course, be acknowledged, and the session utilizes the concept of family relationships as a metaphor for the Jewish people's relationship with Israel: just as families are inextricably tied by enduring bonds over time despite the difficulties encountered at any given moment, the Jewish people are tied to Israel by enduring bonds over time, no matter what the challenges of any given moment may be. The Set Induction is designed to convey this concept quite directly.

Text study is utilized to help participants develop a clear understanding of our people's relationship with the Land of Israel since the beginning of our history, with Zionism as an important modern day development. The shift from the biblical vision to the modern one is also used as a parallel to good parenting practice, which moves children from dependence to independence in a loving, supportive way. Finally, participants will be asked to develop their own Israel Connection Action Plans that they can take home and discuss with their children.

Enduring Understanding

Nurturing a strong Jewish identity requires the active participation of parents in their children's Jewish living and learning experiences.

Essential Questions

1. Who am I as a Jewish parent and a Jewish role model?
2. How does one establish a sacred relationship between parent and child?
3. What makes a meaningful Jewish life?
4. What does it mean to be a Jewish family?

Questions to Be Addressed

1. What can we learn about the Jewish people's relationship with Israel from biblical texts?
2. How do we as contemporary Jews understand our relationship to Israel today?
3. How do we foster in our children a positive connection to the Land of Israel?

Evidence of Understanding

- Participants will discuss biblical texts that focus on the Jewish people's connection to the Land of Israel.
- Participants will create an Israel Connection Action Plan that describes the steps they will take to strengthen their family's connection to Israel.

Session Overview

- Set Induction (15 minutes)
- Text Study and Time Line (30–40 minutes)
- Zionism as a Parenting Model (20 minutes)
- Conclusion (15 minutes)

Materials Needed

- Index cards and a pen or pencil for each participant
- Photocopies of texts, time line, and worksheets (pages 53–58)
- Chalkboard and chalk or flip chart and markers

SESSION PLAN

Set Induction (15 minutes)

The goal of this Set Induction is to help participants understand that difficult moments in the life of a family are balanced by the larger context of commitment. This will be used as a metaphor through which we can understand our relationship to Israel over time.

1. Distribute to each participant an index card and a pen.
2. Ask each participant to think of a particularly difficult moment that occurred in his or her family and to describe it, in a sentence or two, on the index card. Mention that participants will not be asked to share with others what they have written if they choose not to.

3. When they have written their sentences, ask the participants to think about what motivated them to try to address the challenge, and to write that down on the other side of the index card.

4. When the group is ready, ask participants to share what they wrote on the reverse side of the index card; that is, what was the motivation to address the challenge? If possible, record some or all of the answers to this question on the board or flip chart. (These might include: *I realized how much I love my teenager even though I was angry; when we were facing bankruptcy, I thought it was all over but then I realized there are more important things about this family than money; etc.*)

5. Reflect on and summarize the answers given. Explain to the participants that, just as family members have good reasons for solving their problems because they are committed to each over time, the Jewish people have an eternal relationship with Israel that supercedes the challenges of any given moment. Tell the participants that in this session, they will be exploring that relationship and its meaning for us today as Jews and as parents.

Text Study and Time Line (30–40 minutes)

In this activity, participants will examine texts that reflect the attitudes and feelings of the Jewish people toward Israel throughout our history.

1. Divide the group into smaller groups of three or four people each, and distribute the handouts on pages 53–58.

2. Ask participants to turn to the Israel Connection Text Study sheet on page 53 and ask each group to discuss the texts and to answer the questions that follow them.

3. Reconvene the whole group and facilitate a discussion of participant reactions to the texts and invite each group to share its responses to the questions.

Zionism as a Parenting Model (20 minutes)

1. Review the time line on page 56 with the participants. In particular, ask them to compare the amount of time the Jewish people has spent in the Land compared to the amount of time we have spent in exile. You may want to mention that this time line is taken from the *CHAI Level 5 Curriculum Core,* and as such is written for young children, not adults.

2. Ask participants to reflect back on the first biblical text they studied in this session. Invite them to offer possible answers to this question: If God promised the land to Abraham and his descendants, why have we been in exile for so much of our history? Allow for about 10 minutes of discussion.

3. Share with participants a traditional explanation often given for this situation: We were exiled from the Land in punishment for our sins; we have not been worthy of living in the Land.

4. Ask participants to consider the more modern Zionist response that shifts responsibility to us for making Israel a reality in our lives: "If you will it, it is no dream" (Theodor Herzl). Invite discussion about the difference between the two ideas and, if possible, suggest the empowering nature of Zionism, which challenges each generation to fulfill the biblical vision.

5. Ask the participants to think about their own parenting in terms of a continuum: how might they want the relationship between parent and child to shift over time? *(From dependence to independence.)* Ask them to compare this shift in parenting responsibility to the shift in responsibility for the establishment/maintenance of a Jewish homeland from God to us, as suggested by the biblical and modern texts. Invite reactions to this concept.

Conclusion (15 minutes)

1. Ask participants to turn to Ways to Learn About and Support Israel (page 57).
2. Go over the suggestions with participants and ask if they have any additional ideas.
3. Ask participants to complete the Israel Connection Action Plan on page 58. Ask if there are any questions about it.
4. Ask the group to reflect upon their learning at this session and to share one new thing they learned about Israel today.

Israel Connection Text Study

From the Torah

The Lord said to Abram, "Go forth from your native land and from your father's house to the land that I will show you. And I will make of you a great nation, and I will bless you."

(GENESIS 12:1-2)

Discussion Questions

1. What links Abram (who will later be known as Abraham) to the Land?
2. What has been promised to him?
3. What has been promised to his offspring?
4. If we are the children of Abraham, what is our connection to the Land?
5. Do you agree or disagree with the following: Our connection to the Land is deeper and more meaningful because it is part of our spiritual heritage—promised to the Jewish people by God. Explain.

From the Prophets

And there is hope for your future, says the Lord, and your children shall come back again to their own border.

(JEREMIAH 31:16)

And God promised: "I will take you from among the nations and gather you from all the countries, and I will bring you back to your own land. Then you shall dwell in the land which I gave to your ancestors and you shall be My people, and I shall be your God."

(EZEKIEL 36:24, 28)

Discussion Questions

1. Can you describe the feeling behind these texts?

2. What do you think might have been happening to the Jewish people, based on these words?

From Reform Rabbis

We are privileged to live in an extraordinary time, one in which a third Jewish commonwealth has been established in our people's ancient homeland. . . . We have both a stake and a responsibility in building the State of Israel, assuring its security, and defining its Jewish character.

(CENTRAL CONFERENCE ON AMERICAN RABBIS, "REFORM JUDAISM: A CENTENARY PERSPECTIVE [1976]" IN *THE REFORM JUDAISM READER,* ED. MICHAEL A. MEYER AND W. GUNTHER PLAUT [NEW YORK: UAHC PRESS, 2001], P. 206)

We affirm that both Israeli and Diaspora Jewry should remain vibrant and interdependent communities. As we urge Jews who reside outside Israel to learn Hebrew as a living language and to make periodic visits to Israel in order to study and to deepen their relationship to the Land and its people, so do we affirm that Israeli Jews have much to learn from the religious life of Diaspora Jewish communities.

(CENTRAL CONFERENCE OF AMERICAN RABBIS, "A STATEMENT OF PRINCIPLES FOR REFORM JUDAISM [1999]" IN *THE REFORM JUDAISM READER,* ED. MICHAEL A. MEYER AND W. GUNTHER PLAUT [NEW YORK: UAHC PRESS, 2001], P. 212)

Discussion Questions

1. What do these texts say about the Reform movement's commitment to the modern State of Israel?

2. Are the feelings expressed in these texts meaningful for you? Do they reflect your own beliefs and connections to Israel? Explain.

From Reform Movement Prayer Books

Guardian of Israel and Redeemer of all the world, grant that Zion may become a light to the nations. Give its people strength to build a land in which the vision of justice and mercy shall be fulfilled for the good of all the world.

(*GATES OF PRAYER: THE NEW UNION PRAYERBOOK* [NEW YORK: CENTRAL CONFERENCE OF AMERICAN RABBIS, 1975], P. 414)

We pray for the Land of Israel and all its people. May its borders know peace, its inhabitants tranquility. And may the bonds of faith and fate which unite the Jews of all lands be a source of strength to Israel and to us all. God of all lands and ages, answer our constant prayer with a Zion once more aglow with light for us and all the world, and let us say, Amen.

(*MISHKAN T'FILAH: THE NEW REFORM SIDDUR. SHABBAT MORNING* [DRAFT] [NEW YORK: CENTRAL CONFERENCE OF AMERICAN RABBIS, 2002], P. 107)

Discussion Questions

1. How do the words from our prayer books reflect the hopes of the Jewish people with regard to Israel?

2. Do the hopes expressed reflect your own hopes? Why or why not?

Jewish History and the Land of Israel Time Line

(from the *CHAI Level 5 Curriculum Core*)

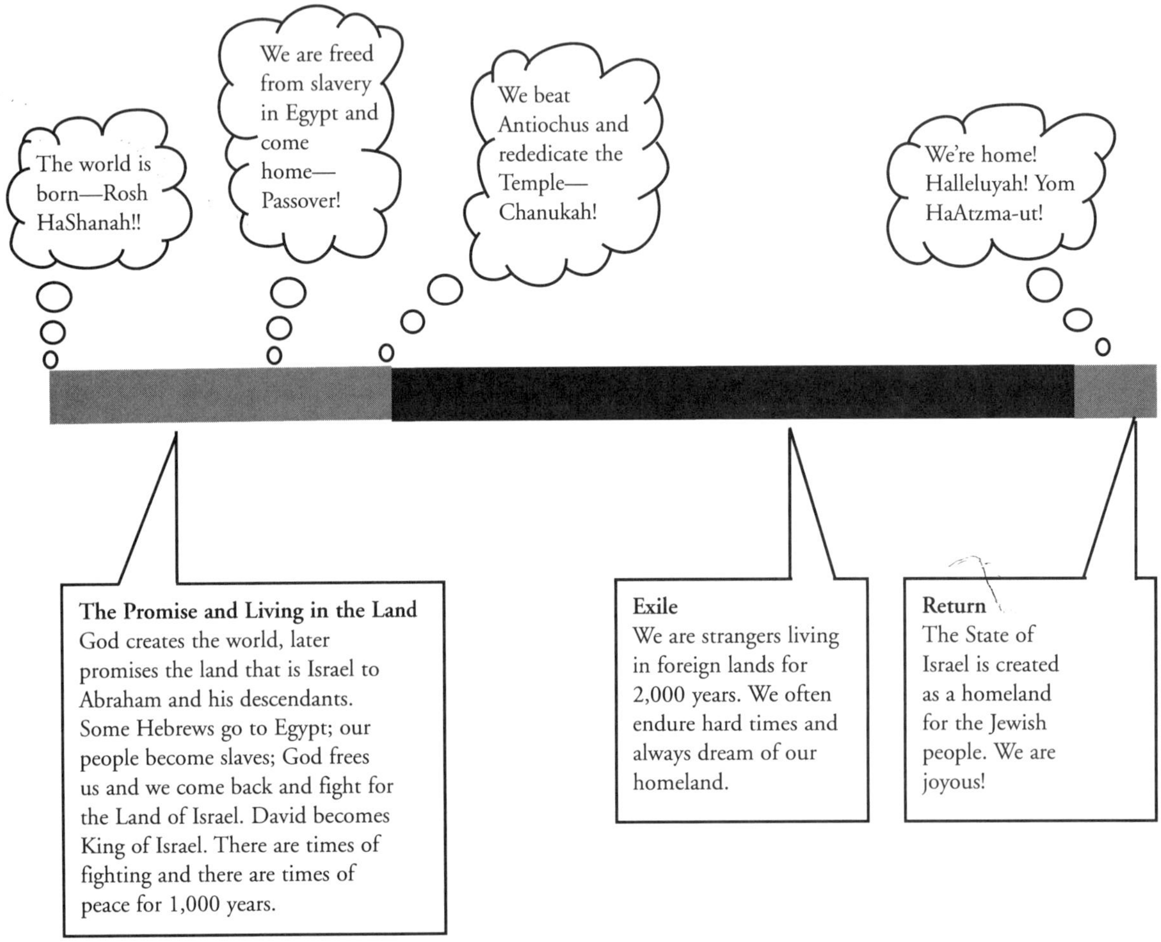

Ways to Learn About and Support Israel

- Visit Web sites:

  www.virtualjerusalem.com (Virtual Jerusalem—news and resources on Israel and Judaism)
  www.camera.org (Committee for Accuracy in Middle East Reporting in America)
  www.jpost.com (*Jerusalem Post* newspaper—English language daily)
  www.haaretzdaily.com (*Ha'aretz* newspaper—English edition)
  www.israelnews2.co.il (Israeli TV News)
  www.mfa.gov.il (Israeli Ministry of Foreign Affairs)

- Go to Israel. Discuss and plan a family trip to Israel.
- Educate yourself about the current political situation in Israel so that you can answer any questions your child might have.
- Make use of the temple library for appropriate family resources on Israel.
- Incorporate conversation about Israel into your holiday celebrations.
- Give to causes that support Israel and its citizens.
- Help Israel's economy by purchasing Israeli products. (You can shop direct by visiting **www.shopinisrael.com**.)

Israel Connection Action Plan

Using the Ways to Learn About and Support Israel list, pick three or four things you and your family can do soon to strengthen your Israel connection. Write them here:

	Things We Can Do Soon	When We Will Do Them
1.	________________	________________
2.	________________	________________
3.	________________	________________

Other Ideas

________________	________________
________________	________________
________________	________________

Torah Session 6
What the Four Children of the Passover Seder Can Teach Us About Parenting

INTRODUCTION

Who are the Four Children of the Passover seder and what can they teach us about parenting? The images of the Four Children—the wise, the wicked, the simple, and the one who does not know how to ask—play a pivotal role in the celebration of the Passover seder. The Four Children not only describe ancient temperaments of children, but also shed light on the temperaments of children today. This session includes study and discussion on the biblical verses that provide the textual basis for the Four Children of the Passover seder, examination of the rabbinic interpretations of the Four Children, and sharing of personal responses.

ENDURING UNDERSTANDING

Nurturing a strong Jewish identity requires the active participation of parents in their children's Jewish living and learning experiences.

ESSENTIAL QUESTIONS

1. Who am I as a Jewish parent and a Jewish role model?
2. How does one establish a sacred relationship between parent and child?
3. What makes a meaningful Jewish life?
4. What does it mean to be a Jewish family?

QUESTIONS TO BE ADDRESSED

1. Who are the Four Children of the Passover seder?
2. How did the Rabbis interpret the personalities of the Four Children?
3. How do labels applied to children affect how parents and society respond to them?

4. How did the Rabbis suggest parents respond to each of the Four Children?

5. In what ways are the Four Children of the Passover seder like today's children?

6. What can you learn about parenting from the Four Children?

Evidence of Understanding

- Participants will be able to identify and describe the Four Children of the Passover seder.
- Participants will discuss how to apply the lessons learned about the Four Children of the Passover seder to their own children and their own parenting.

Session Overview

- Set Induction (15 minutes)
- Text Study (40–45 minutes)
- Discussion (15 minutes)
- Conclusion (10 minutes)

Materials Needed

- Chalkboard and chalk or flip chart and markers
- Photocopies of texts and take home materials (pages 63–66)

SESSION PLAN

Set Induction (15 minutes)

1. Divide a chalkboard or flip chart page into four columns.

2. Ask the participants for the descriptive name of each of the Four Children of the Passover seder. Place one descriptive name in each column. Ask the participants, based solely on the descriptive name given to each child of the Passover seder, to suggest synonyms for those labels. Write the participant responses in the appropriate columns. If the participants are initially unable to answer, begin by mentioning one of the children, which will hopefully trigger the rest of the responses. (For example, *the wise child: knowledgeable, sensible, intelligent; the wicked child: rebellious, evil; the simple child: naïve, unassuming; the child who does not know how to ask: unworldly, innocent.*)

3. Discuss the following questions:

   - What are your reactions to the labels given to the Four Children of the Passover seder and the synonyms for those labels?

- How might those labels affect the ways in which one would relate to the child described?
- How do the synonyms broaden your view of the Four Children?

Text Study (40–45 minutes)

1. Introduce the text study by sharing the following with the participants:

   When the Rabbis were assembling the Haggadah, they relied on the text of the Torah to guide them. They found four verses that referred to the obligation to retell the story of the Exodus to our children. According to tradition, nothing superfluous is written in the Torah. If we are instructed four times to teach this story to our children, there must be a reason for mentioning it four times. The evolution of the Four Children is derived from these four Torah verses. The Jerusalem Talmud records that it was Rabbi Hiyya who formulated the questions and responses for the Four Children of the Passover Haggadah. In this parent session, commentary from the two Talmuds, the Babylonian and the Jerusalem, are included with the text material. Both the Babylonian and Jerusalem Talmuds contain the Mishnah, which is the written version of the Oral Law and subsequent commentary by rabbis and sages. The Oral Law includes those laws that by tradition were given to Moses by God orally and then spoken by Moses to the people, but were not written down. Fearing that these laws would be lost if kept only in an oral tradition, they were eventually written down. In *Jewish Literacy,* Rabbi Joseph Telushkin points out that Conservative and Reform Jews see the oral law as an "evolving system, in which successive generations of rabbis discussed and debated how to incorporate the Torah into their lives."[1] Thus they are more apt to modify and change the oral law. The Babylonian Talmud contains the Mishnah and comments of the Rabbis of Babylonia. The Jerusalem Talmud contains the Mishnah and the comments of the Rabbis of the Land of Israel. The Jerusalem Talmud is sometimes referred to as the Palestinian Talmud, since the Land was called Palestine at the time of the Talmud's compilation.

2. Distribute copies of the texts and discussion questions on pages 63–66 to the participants. Read through the texts for each of the Four Children and discuss the questions that follow.

Discussion (15 minutes)

Return to the list of synonyms that were generated in the initial activity of this session. Discuss the following questions:

- Now that you have studied the Four Children, are there other synonyms that you would suggest be added to this list?
- What do you think the labels applied to the Four Children mean? How do labels hurt or help children? What do these labels and synonyms mean for you and your children? What do they mean for your own parenting?

[1]Joseph Telushkin, *Jewish Literacy* (New York: William Morrow and Company, 1991), p. 150.

Conclusion (10 minutes)

1. Share with participants:

   The Four Children of the Passover seder can be seen as a description of four developmental stages through which a child passes: the mature teenager who is ready to ask sophisticated, meaningful questions about Judaism; a younger, rebellious teen who rejects the tradition; a child who becomes interested when he or she sees the preparations for the seder; and a toddler who cannot yet ask questions.[2]

   We can also look at the Four Children as different children, who remind us to consider individual learning styles, abilities, and personalities when educating our children. This part of the seder reminds us that each child is important to our community and is to be instructed in the appropriate manner for him or her.

2. Discuss the following questions:

   - The Rabbis refer to four types of children that a parent might be faced with during the observance of the Passover seder: one wise, one wicked, one simple, and one who does not know how to ask. Can you identify moments when your children were wise, wicked, simple, or did not know how to ask? How have you responded to them in the past? Do you want to change any of those responses in the future? Explain.
   - What benefits are there when a parent can determine from what "stage" or "temperament" a child is behaving?
   - Our children are unique human beings with loving and exasperating qualities, just like the children of the Passover seder. The Rabbis counseled responding to the child in the way the child needed to be responded to. As parents it is our job to nurture the whole child and to look beyond labels and temporary attitudes. What advice would you give to a parent who wants or needs to look beyond a label or stage and to see the whole child?

3. Send participants home with the take-home activity on page 66.

---

[2]Judith Z. Abrams and Steven A. Abrams, *Jewish Parenting, Rabbinic Insights* (Northvale, N.J.: Jason Aronson, Inc., 1994), pp. 148–152.

Text Study

The Wise Child

The wise child asks, "What are the rulings, the laws and the traditions which God has commanded us?" (Deuteronomy 6:20).

According to the Jerusalem Talmud:

We answer: "With a strong hand, God took us out of Egypt, out of the house of bondage" (Exodus 13:14).

According to the Babylonian Talmud:

"You instruct this one in the precepts of Passover, including: One must not continue to feast after the sharing of the afikoman.*"*

Discussion Questions

1. Why would this child be thought of as wise?
2. Which answer—the one from the Jerusalem Talmud or from the Babylonian Talmud—would you choose to give to the wise child? Why?
3. Have your children displayed wisdom? In what ways? Share how you have responded to that wisdom.

The Wicked Child

The wicked child asks, "What is this observance to you?" (Exodus 12:26).

"What bother is this, that you trouble us with, year after year?"

According to the Jerusalem Talmud:

We answer: "to you" and not "to him," "to you" and not "to her." Jews who say "to you" rather than to "to us" remove themselves from the community, and thus reject an essential tenet of our tradition. You should give such people a sharp answer and set their teeth on edge, saying, "Because of what God did for me when I came out of Egypt" (Exodus 13:8). "For me" and not "for them." For if they had been there, they would not have been redeemed.[1]

Discussion Questions

1. Usually the label applied to this child is wicked. What if the label were changed? Take wicked out of the sentence and replace it with one of the synonyms suggested earlier. Does your response or understanding of this child change if the label is changed? How? Why?

2. How would you respond to the "wicked child" of the seder? What if you thought of the child as rebellious or defiant?

3. The commentary says to answer this child sharply, setting the child's teeth on edge. What do you think that means? Does this feel like an appropriate answer? Why or why not?

4. Were you ever a rebellious (wicked or defiant) child? How did your parents respond to you?

5. Have you ever been confronted by a rebellious child? What has been your response?

The Simple Child

The simple child asks, "What is this?"

According to the Jerusalem Talmud:

Teach this child the laws of Passover, namely, "One must not continue to feast after sharing the afikoman*" (Mishnah P'sachim 10:8).*

According to the Babylonian Talmud:

"With a strong hand, God took us out of Egypt, out of the house of bondage" (Exodus 13:14).

---

[1]Translation from Sue Levi Elwell, ed., *The Open Door: A Passover Haggadah* (New York: Central Conference of American Rabbis, 2002), p. 40.

Discussion Questions

1. What would be another name for this "simple child"? Could it be the curious child?

2. Sometimes parents feel bombarded by questions from their children. Has this ever happened to you? How did you respond?

3. How does the Jerusalem Talmud counsel answering the simple child? Refer to the first word of the response. What is it? How, when, where, and why are parents teachers of their children? What does that mean in terms of parental time and attention? What can be the long-term effects if we take this lesson to heart?

The Child Who Does Not Know How to Ask

According to the Jerusalem Talmud:

It is for you to open this child's mind. Rabbi Jose said, "This is a mishnah, a teaching—If the child has no understanding, the parent must teach the child." You must take the initiative and begin the story for this child yourself as it is written, "You shall tell your child on that day, saying: 'This is because of what **Adonai** ***did for me when I went free from Egypt' " (Exodus 13:8).***

Discussion Questions

1. What is the difference between a "simple child" and a "child who does not know how to ask a question"? Re-examine the text material. What does a "simple child" do that the "child who does not know how to ask a question" does not do?

2. If we think of the "simple child" as a curious child, how can a parent foster curiosity in the "child who does not know how to ask"?

Engaging Your Children in Conversation

1. Most Haggadot contain artistic interpretations of the Four Children. With your family, examine the Haggadah used at your family seder. If you do not own a Haggadah, arrange to borrow one from the synagogue. If it is possible, have copies of three or four different Haggadot. Share with your children that you have been studying the Four Children of the Passover Seder.

2. Examine the illustration of the Four Children. If you are using multiple Haggadot, compare the illustrations. Discuss: Who is depicted? How do you know who is wise, who is rebellious, who is simple, and who does not know how to ask a question?

3. Ask your child how he or she would illustrate the Four Children. Take out drawing supplies and create your own illustrations. Compare and discuss what you each have drawn.

4. Discuss times when you as the parent have felt wise, rebellious, simple, or felt like you did not know how to ask a question. Encourage your child to share similar feelings.

Avodah Session 1 Shabbat: Day of Rest, Day of Wonder, Day of Peace

Introduction

This session focuses on Shabbat and its place in Jewish life. While the Sabbath has always been a central aspect of Jewish identity and observance, for today's fast-paced, over-programmed families, the celebration of Shabbat can have a powerfully restorative impact on family relationships and peace.

Two possible approaches to conducting the session are presented here. Option A utilizes the film *Fiddler on the Roof* as an introduction; in this approach, the idea of Shabbat as timeless in considered. The session begins with a quote from *The Sabbath* by Abraham Joshua Heschel, which sets the framework for viewing the opening ten minutes of *Fiddler on the Roof.* Option B uses an introduction that focuses on the everyday lives of the participants and offers Shabbat as an opportunity for weekly renewal and reconnection. Both options present the concept of Shabbat as a time of rest and recuperation, Shabbat as a gift, and Shabbat as a time of partnership with God.

Since the subject of Shabbat is such an important one, the session contains a great deal of material and much opportunity for participants to share, discuss, and reflect. For this reason, it is recommended that you schedule this as a two-hour session.

Enduring Understanding

Nurturing a strong Jewish identity requires the active participation of parents in their children's Jewish living and learning experiences.

Essential Questions

1. Who am I as a Jewish parent and a Jewish role model?
2. How does one establish a sacred relationship between parent and child?
3. What makes a meaningful Jewish life?
4. What does it mean to be a Jewish family?

Questions to Be Addressed

1. What is the function and purpose of Shabbat?
2. Can I and my family relate to Shabbat and have it become a part of our lives?
3. How can we apply Jewish teachings about Shabbot to our lives and the lives of our families?

Evidence of Understanding

- Participants will be able to discuss Shabbat from four perspectives: as timeless, as rest and recuperation, as a gift, and as a time of partnership with God.
- Participants will relate these four perspectives on Shabbat to themselves and to their families.
- Participants will share ways in which they can make Shabbat "a palace in time" for themselves and their families.

Session Overview

- Set Induction (Option A or Option B; 20–25 minutes)
- Midrash Text Study (40–60 minutes)
- Conclusion (10–15 minutes)

Materials Needed

- Video or DVD of *Fiddler on the Roof* (for Option A)
- Photocopies of all texts and The Jewish Parent Page for Shabbat (pages 71–80)

SESSION PLAN

Set Induction (Option A; 20–25 minutes)

1. View the first 10 minutes of the film *Fiddler on the Roof*. This section of the film includes the song "Tradition," which serves as the introduction to the film and occurs before the opening credits. Follow up the video clip by discussing the following questions:
    - Jewish life in the small villages of eastern Europe, called *shtetls* in Yiddish, is often romanticized, presenting visions of an easy, pious Jewish life in a simpler time and place. In reality, life was often a difficult struggle. Based on what you viewed in the opening scenes in *Fiddler on the Roof*, what did the *shtetl* residents wrestle with during the week?

- In the song "Tradition," what does Tevya identify as the anchors in the lives of his family and neighbors? What gives the people balance?
- Fast forwarding to our era, what do you wrestle with during the week? What are your anchors? What gives you balance? What are the similarities between our lives and the lives of the *shtetl* dwellers?

2. Distribute copies of the handouts on pages 71–80, and ask for a volunteer to read aloud the quote from Rabbi Abraham Joshua Heschel on page 71:

   > Six days a week we wrestle with the world, wringing profit from the earth; on the Sabbath we especially care for the seed of eternity planted in the soul. The world has our hands, but our soul belongs to Someone Else.[1]

3. Discuss the following questions:

   - By applying Heschel's text to both our lives and life in the *shtetl,* how is Shabbat an antidote to what is faced during the week?
   - What makes Shabbat timeless?

Set Induction (Option B; 20–25 minutes)

1. Once the participants are assembled and seated, lead them in guided meditation. Ask them to close their eyes and picture in their minds the things that make their lives stressful. Next, ask them to take several deep breaths and remove each of the stress-causers in their lives. They can place these in a mental "trash can."
2. Now, ask the participants to picture what a perfect evening and the following day might look like, removing from the picture activities containing commercial transactions, if possible. They should hold this image for at least 10 seconds.
3. Have the participants take one or two more deep breaths and open their eyes, while retaining the mental picture of the perfect evening and day. Ask them to share with the group the mental images they had during the meditation and write key words on the board or chart paper. (These might include: *intimate time with my partner, reading a book, taking a nature hike, spending quality time with our children, getting together with close friends, etc.*)
4. Distribute the handouts on pages 71–80 to the participants and ask a volunteer to read the text on page 72 aloud:

   > The root of the word Shabbat means to "cease" or "desist." To observe Shabbat means to cease our work life and break our daily routine every seventh day, making that day holy. Shabbat is to be a day of enjoying God's world rather than doing battle with it; a day of relaxation rather than struggle, a time to live in harmony rather than to achieve domination.[2]

---

[1]Abraham Joshua Heschel, *The Sabbath* (New York: Farrar, Straus and Giroux, 1951), p. 13.
[2]Arthur Green, *These Are the Words: A Vocabulary of Jewish Spiritual Life* (Woodstock, Vt.: Jewish Lights Publishing, 1999), p. 255.

5. Ask the participants to compare their thoughts about the perfect day with this definition written by Rabbi Arthur Green. How does it compare? Explain that in this session, the participants will be exploring the value of setting aside one day each week to create, as best they can, the "perfect" day that the Jewish people call Shabbat.

Midrash Text Study (40–60 minutes)

1. Tell participants that they will now study some midrashim about Shabbat. Explain that midrashim are stories and explanations of biblical verses meant to help us gain greater understanding of the meaning of the text, beyond what is explicitly described in the text.

2. Divide the participants into groups of four. Ask participants to study Shabbat Text 1 on page 73 and discuss the questions. When 10 to 15 minutes have elapsed, ask the groups to rearrange themselves so new groups of four are created, and direct them to study Shabbat Text 2. Repeat this procedure for Texts 3 and 4.

3. Reconvene as one large group. Ask the participants to complete the following sentence:

   "I can build a palace in time for my family when I ________________."

Conclusion (10–15 minutes)

1. Ask participants to share any new insights or understandings they may have experienced as a result of their participation in today's session.

2. Review What Is Shabbat? (page 76) with the participants and invite their reactions.

3. Distribute copies of The Jewish Parent Page for Shabbat (pages 77–80). This is a publication of the Union for Reform Judaism and can be found on the Union Web site, along with other Jewish Parent Pages, at **www.urj.org/educate/parent/**.

Abraham Joshua Heschel on Shabbat

Six days a week we wrestle with the world, wringing profit from the earth; on the Sabbath we especially care for the seed of eternity planted in the soul. The world has our hands, but our soul belongs to Someone Else.

(ABRAHAM JOSHUA HESCHEL, *THE SABBATH* [NEW YORK: FARRAR, STRAUS AND GIROUX, 1951], P. 13)

Discussion Questions

1. By applying Heschel's text to both our lives and life in the *shtetl,* how is Shabbat an antidote to what is faced during the week?

2. What makes Shabbat timeless?

Arthur Green on Shabbat

The root of the word Shabbat means to "cease" or "desist." To observe Shabbat means to cease our work life and break our daily routine every seventh day, making that day holy. Shabbat is to be a day of enjoying God's world rather than doing battle with it; a day of relaxation rather than struggle, a time to live in harmony rather than to achieve domination.

(ARTHUR GREEN, *THESE ARE THE WORDS: A VOCABULARY OF JEWISH SPIRITUAL LIFE* [WOODSTOCK, VT.: JEWISH LIGHTS PUBLISHING, 1999], P. 255)

Text Study

Shabbat Text 1

"Moses went out to his kinfolk and witnessed their toil" (Exodus 2:11).

The Rabbis teach, "Moses saw that the Hebrews had no rest from their labor. He therefore went to Pharaoh and said to him, 'If one has a slave and he does not allow the slave to rest at least one day in the week, the slave is apt to die from exhaustion. These Hebrews are your slaves. If you do not let them rest one day in the week they too may die.' Thereupon Pharaoh said to Moses, 'Go and do unto them as you have suggested.' So Moses went and established for them the Sabbath as a day of rest and recuperation."

(*SH'MOT RABBAH* 1:28)

Discussion Questions

1. What are your needs for rest and recuperation?
2. What kinds of boundaries regarding work make sense for you and your family?
3. How would your family benefit from Shabbat rest and recuperation?
4. What are the challenges you and your family face in creating boundaries between everyday pursuits and Shabbat?

Shabbat Text 2

"Speak to the Israelite people and say: . . . you must keep My Sabbaths, for this is a sign between Me and you throughout the ages, that you may know that I, Adonai, *have consecrated you" (Exodus 31:13).*

On this verse the Rabbis of the Talmud taught, "The Holy One of blessing said to Moses, 'I have a precious gift in My treasure house, and its name is Shabbat. I wish to present it to Israel. Go and make it known to them.'"

(TALMUD, *SHABBAT* 10B)

Discussion Questions

1. How do you feel when you give a gift? What do you expect from the recipient?
2. How do you want or expect your children to respond to a gift they get and/or receive?
3. What would it mean to give your children the gift of Shabbat?

Shabbat Text 3

"And the heaven and the earth were finished and all their array. On the seventh day God finished the work . . . and God ceased" (Genesis 2:1–2).

Rabbi Hamnuna taught: "The one who prays on the eve of the Sabbath and recites the verses that begin, 'and the heaven and the earth were finished,' the Scriptures speaks of that person as though he or she had become a partner with the Holy One of blessing, in the Creation." The Rabbis of the Talmud suggested reading the biblical text not as Va-yechullu*—and the heaven and the earth were finished—but as* Va-yechallu*—and they* finished the creation of the heaven and the earth.*

(TALMUD, *SHABBAT* 119B)

Discussion Questions

1. What did God do once Creation was completed?
2. What does it mean to understand humans as partners with God in creation? How can we translate that into our own lives?

* "they" meaning God and humankind.

3. In *Fiddler on the Roof,* Tevye says, "And because of our traditions everyone of us knows who he is and what God expects him to do." As co-creators with God, what do you think God expects of us in relation to Shabbat?

Shabbat Text 4

The seventh day is a palace in time which we build.

(ABRAHAM JOSHUA HESCHEL, *THE SABBATH* [NEW YORK: FARRAR, STRAUS AND GIROUX, 1951], P. 15)

Discussion Question

◆ What would constitute a palace in time for your family?

One thing our family can do right away to build a palace in time on Shabbat is ______________________________________.

What Is Shabbat?

- Encouragement to experience Jewish ritual every week.
- Quality time that you set aside for the appreciation of yourself, your loved ones, your friends, and your environment.
- A time to eat, drink, and be merry.
- An opportunity to be part of a spiritual community and an opportunity to grow as an individual.
- A chance to be thankful for the blessings you have and to pray for the things that truly matter.
- Your weekly "birthday party" for the world; a celebration of the joys of living, loving, and creativity; a time to sing![1]

Shabbat enables us to gain perspective, to reflect on what we have done, and to notice what still needs to be done. For Shabbat is first of all a haven from the week. Especially in our modern world, it reminds us to stop worrying about our accomplishments, about "getting somewhere" or about "being someone." Shabbat shows that meaning in our lives lies not in what we have accomplished but in being part of the universe. It provides both time and opportunity to rediscover ourselves.

(MICHAEL STRASSFELD, *A BOOK OF LIFE: EMBRACING JUDAISM AS A SPIRITUAL PRACTICE* [NEW YORK: SCHOCKEN BOOKS, INC., 2002], P. 103)

[1]Adapted from Ruth Perelson, *An Invitation to Shabbat* (New York: UAHC Press, 1997), pp. vii–viii.

UNION FOR REFORM JUDAISM

Winter 2004 • Choref 5764

The Jewish Parent Page

SHABBAT • Day of Joy, Day of Gladness, Day of Peace

Holiday Schedule

Shabbat arrives every Friday evening at sundown and ends when three stars appear in the Saturday night sky. Many consider Shabbat the most sacred of Jewish holidays. It is a special gift for the Jewish people, giving us the opportunity for meaningful rest, celebration and prayer.

Check with your local synagogue for a schedule of services.

Meanings and Observances

In the Torah we read, "And the heaven and the earth were finished and all their array. On the seventh day God finished the work that He had been doing, and He ceased on the seventh day from all the work that He had done." (Genesis 2:1-2)

Jewish tradition asks us to emulate God on the Sabbath day—just as God ceased working and rested, so we too cease working and rest. Whether we believe in a literal God of creation, a God who set into motion the evolution of the world, or another interpretation of how God works in our world, we set aside one day each week to celebrate the magnificence of creation and our partnership with God. In celebrating Shabbat, we reach out toward holiness while God is reaching out to us.

- **Shabbat Preparation**: It is a tradition to prepare both our homes and ourselves for Shabbat by making sure our homes are clean before Shabbat begins and by dressing in clothes that honor Shabbat. These preparations help create a peaceful and calm atmosphere for the celebration of Shabbat.
- **Setting the Table**: Candles are placed in candlesticks, wine or juice is poured into *Kiddush* cups (special decorative cups or wine goblets), and a challah with a challah cover is placed on the table.
- **Sabbath Home Ceremony**: When the family gathers at the table, a blessing is said over the candles, wine or juice, and challah. Additionally, a blessing is said over the children.
- **The Candles**: There are many interpretations as to why we light candles. A comment found in the Zohar (a medieval work of mystical Judaism) teaches that when the table is set, the candles lit, and family members are happy, the *Shechinah*—the Divine Presence—dwells within the home. The candles set the tone for the holiday to begin.
- **The Wine**: The blessing over the wine is called *Kiddush*. The word *Kiddush* means sanctification. We sanctify Shabbat by the blessings we say. Wine is associated with joy and celebration. The rabbis of the talmudic period established the tradition of sanctifying the Sabbath through the blessing over the wine.
- **The Challah**: Typically a challah is a braided loaf of bread. The blessing over the challah is called *HaMotzi*. *HaMotzi* means "to bring forth." When we bless the challah or bread, we thank God for bringing forth bread from the earth. The challah is covered with a cloth; it can be a napkin or a specially decorated cloth for the specific purpose of covering the challah. Different explanations have been given for the use of the challah cover. One

Continued on next page

interpretation is that the challah is covered so that it is not "embarrassed" by being blessed after the wine and not before it. Another explanation is that the challah represents the breads that would have been given to the priests as an offering in the Temple in Jerusalem. These breads would have been placed on the altar upon a beautiful cloth. Since the destruction of the Temple, our homes have come to represent the Temple in miniature, and the table upon which we eat the altar. Some families have two challot (pl. of challah) on Friday evening, commemorating the double portion of manna that God provided the Children of Israel on Fridays during their journey from Egypt to the Promised Land.

- **The Friday Evening Meal**: Many families prepare a special Friday evening meal, which may be take-out food from a restaurant, pre-made dishes from the grocery store or home cooking. The ritual candles, wine and challah create the atmosphere of the Sabbath table.
- **Shabbat Services, Evening and Morning**: Synagogue services are usually held on *Erev Shabbat* (the evening of the Sabbath) and on Shabbat morning. Check with your local synagogue for the schedule of services, including any special worship services for families with children. As a family, become part of your community's Shabbat worship. In addition to the benefits of praying together, participating capably and communally in holiday observance will help your children see the relevance of what they study in religious school.
- **Shabbat Meals**: In addition to the Friday evening meal, all the meals eaten on Shabbat are (and can be) special meals. For many busy families, it is better to have guests at lunchtime on Shabbat than at the end of a busy workday.
- **Shabbat Rest**: The rest we observe on Shabbat is meant to be unique. Rest on Shabbat should be both physically and spiritually restoring. Rest on Shabbat includes festive meals, prayer, and time together with family and friends.
- ***Havdalah***: Observe the ceremony of *Havdalah*, which signifies the end of the Sabbath. *Havdalah* is celebrated once there are three stars visible in the night sky. An explanation of *Havdalah* along with a *Havdalah* ceremony and additional family activities can be found archived on The Jewish Parent Page website: **www.urj.org/educate/parent/0305.shtml**.

Teach Your Children Well...the mitzvot and ethics of Jewish life

There are four mitzvot associated with Shabbat. These mitzvot are derived from four verses found in the Bible:

"*Remember* the Sabbath day to keep it holy." (Exodus 20:8)

"*Observe* the Sabbath day to keep it holy." (Deuteronomy 5:12)

"...if you call the Sabbath '*delight*,' God's holy day '*honored*'; and if you honor it and go not your ways, nor look to your affairs, nor strike bargains; then you can delight in God." (Isaiah 58:13-14)

To fulfill the commandments to (1) remember, (2) observe, (3) delight in, and (4) honor Shabbat, the rabbis specified certain actions–such as refraining from work, lighting the candles, eating delicious meals, and dressing in special clothing.

With your children, generate ideas and family activities that will fulfill these four mitzvot:

As a family we can *remember* Shabbat by ______________________________

As a family we can *observe* Shabbat by ______________________________

As a family we can *honor* and *delight* in Shabbat by ______________________________

Here are a few ideas to get you started:

- It is a tradition to give *tzedakah* before Shabbat begins. Usually this means that family members place a few coins in a *tzedakah* box. With your family, generate a list of worthy causes.
- Choose Jewish-themed books and/or music to share at Shabbat bedtime or during the day with your children.
- Spend time out in nature on Shabbat by taking a family walk outside and/or having a Shabbat picnic.

A Jewish Family's Bookshelf

From the UAHC Press and Transcontinental Music

www.uahcpress.com

Celebrate Shabbat (CD) Produced by Craig Taubman

A treasure of Sabbath songs from some of contemporary Jewish music's most beloved musical artists—listen to MP3 samples on the UAHC Press website!

CHAI Jewish Family Education: Shabbat Family Workbook By Michelle Shapiro Abraham, illustrated by Lisa Rauchwerger

Family activities, discussion guides, recipes, blessings and songs.

Do It Yourself Shabbat

Blessings for *Erev Shabbat* (Friday night) on a laminated fold-out card

An Invitation to Shabbat: A Beginner's Guide to Weekly Celebration (with CD) By Ruth Perelson

A step-by-step guide to Shabbat rituals from candle lighting to *Havdalah*

Shaarei Shabbat: Songs and Blessings for Your Jewish Home (CD) Produced by Doug Cotler

Folk melodies, contemporary classics and synagogue standards sung by cantors and soloists, with a track list and MP3 samples available on the UAHC Press website

The Shabbat Angels By Maxine Segal Handelman, Illustrated by Joani Keller Rothenberg

A contemporary version of a talmudic tale teaching the value of Shabbat peace

A Shabbat Reader: Universe of Cosmic Joy By Dov Peretz Elkins

A collection of spiritual essays, poetry, and meditations on the transcendent meaning of the seventh day, with an online discussion guide

Shabbat Shalom! By Michelle Shapiro Abraham and illustrated by Ann Koffsky

A wonderful way to teach toddlers about lighting Shabbat candles, reciting the *Kiddush*, saying the blessing over the challah and more

Shabbat Shalom! Jewish Children's Songs and Blessings for Shabbat (CD)

A companion to the book of the same name, suitable for newborns to six-year-olds, with track list and MP3 samples available on the website

Recipe Corner

Yummy Sabbath Crescents

A quick and easy Shabbat treat

Ingredients:

1 8 oz. can refrigerated crescent roll dough

1/3-cup brown sugar

2 teaspoons cinnamon

Raisins, optional

Directions:
Preheat oven to 375°F.

Open the container of crescent roll dough and separate the dough triangles. Arrange the dough triangles on an un-greased cookie sheet.

Blend the brown sugar and cinnamon. Spread this filling on each triangle.

If desired, sprinkle 4-5 raisins down the middle of the dough.

Roll up the dough triangles beginning with the wide end and rolling toward the point.

Bake for approximately 10 minutes or until golden brown.

Transfer the baked rolls onto a wire rack to cool.

Allow rolls to cool before enjoying the treat. Makes 8 rolls.

Optional: Blend 1/4 cup of confectioners sugar with 1 teaspoon milk. Drizzle over the Yummy Sabbath Crescents as they are cooling. Enjoy warm or at room temperature.

Gathering Around the Shabbat Table

Hadlakat neirot: The Blessing over the Shabbat Candles

Kindle the Shabbat candles (typically 2 candles), and chant or recite:

בָּרוּךְ אַתָּה יי אֱלֹהֵינוּ מֶלֶךְ הָעוֹלָם אֲשֶׁר קִדְּשָׁנוּ
בְּמִצְוֹתָיו וְצִוָּנוּ לְהַדְלִיק נֵר שֶׁל שַׁבָּת.

Baruch atah Adonai, Eloheinu melech ha-olam asher kid'shanu b'mitzvotav v'tzivanu l'hadlik neir shel Shabbat.

We praise you, Eternal God, Sovereign of the Universe, who makes us holy with mitzvot and commands us to kindle the Sabbath lights.

Blessing the Children

Place your hands on your child's head and say:

For boys:

יְשִׂמְךָ אֱלֹהִים כְּאֶפְרַיִם וְכִמְנַשֶּׁה.

Y'simcha Elohim k'Ephrayim v'chiM'nasheh.

May God inspire you to live in the tradition of Ephraim and Menasheh, who carried forward the life of our people.

For girls:

יְשִׂמֵךְ אֱלֹהִים כְּשָׂרָה, רִבְקָה, לֵאָה, וְרָחֵל.

Y'simeich Elohim k'Sarah, Rivkah, Lei-ah, v'Rachel.

May God inspire you to live in the tradition of Sarah, Rebecca, Leah and Rachel, who carried forward the life of our people.

For both:

יְבָרֶכְךָ יי וְיִשְׁמְרֶךָ.
יָאֵר יי פָּנָיו אֵלֶיךָ וִיחֻנֶּךָּ.
יִשָּׂא יהוה פָּנָיו אֵלֶיךָ וְיָשֵׂם לְךָ שָׁלוֹם.

Y'varech'cha Adonai v'yishm'recha.

Ya-eir Adonai panav eilecha vichuneka.

Yisah Adonai panav eilecha v'yaseim l'cha shalom.

May God bless you and keep you.

May God look kindly upon you, and be gracious to you.

May God reach out to you in tenderness and give you peace.

If you choose, add personal thoughts and blessings.

Kiddush: The Blessing Over the Wine*

Lift the cup(s) of wine or juice and say:

בָּרוּךְ אַתָּה יי אֱלֹהֵינוּ מֶלֶךְ הָעוֹלָם, בּוֹרֵא פְּרִי הַגָּפֶן.

Baruch atah Adonai, Eloheinu melech ha-olam, borei p'ri hagafen.

We praise You, Eternal God, Sovereign of the Universe, who creates the fruit of the vine.

Drink the wine or juice.

(*For the full text, see *On the Doorposts of Your House*, CCAR Press.)

HaMotzi: The Blessing Over the Bread

Uncover the challah and say:

בָּרוּךְ אַתָּה יי אֱלֹהֵינוּ מֶלֶךְ הָעוֹלָם, הַמּוֹצִיא לֶחֶם מִן הָאָרֶץ

Baruch atah Adonai, Eloheinu melech ha-olam, hamotzi lechem min ha-aretz.

We praise You, Eternal God, Sovereign of the universe, who brings forth bread from the earth.

Cut or break off pieces of challah for each family member to eat.

Enjoy your Sabbath meal.

The Jewish Parent Page is a publication of the Union for Reform Judaism and is written by Barbara Binder Kadden, R.J.E., regional educator for the Pacific Central West Council. Bkadden@urj.org

WWW.URJ.ORG/EDUCATE/PARENT • 212.650.4110 • EDUCATE@URJ.ORG

Avodah Session 2
Blessing Our Children: Building Connection, Building Love

INTRODUCTION

In *Jewish Living: A Guide to Contemporary Reform Practice,* Rabbi Mark Washofsky writes, "It is a mitzvah for parents to bless their children at the Shabbat (and holiday) table each week."[1] Blessing children is a loving custom that binds one generation to the next with affection, love, and care. *Birkat Y'ladim* is recited on Friday evening and on holidays. This blessing is recited just after the kindling and blessing of the Shabbat or holiday candles. The parent places his or her hands on the head of the child to be blessed and recites the blessings. Many parents are not aware of this practice, but it has enormous potential for families. It can build bonds of love and connection between parent and child. It can remind us and our children that we are simply thankful that they are in our lives.

There will be extensive small group study and discussion in this session. For the groups' deliberations to be most successful, the session leader should appoint or ask for a volunteer facilitator in each group. That individual will ensure that the group completes its discussion within the time allotted. During this process, the session leader should move among the groups to offer any assistance that may be needed.

Finally, since participants will actually be practicing the *Birkat Y'ladim* blessings in this session, the session leader must either be comfortable reciting and teaching the Hebrew of the blessing or should be certain that another teacher will be present to properly teach the blessings.

ENDURING UNDERSTANDING

Nurturing a strong Jewish identity requires the active participation of parents in their children's Jewish living and learning experiences.

ESSENTIAL QUESTIONS

1. Who am I as a Jewish parent and a Jewish role model?
2. How does one establish a sacred relationship between parent and child?
3. What makes a meaningful Jewish life?
4. What does it mean to be a Jewish family?

[1]Mark Washofsky, *Jewish Living: A Guide to Contemporary Reform Practice* (New York: UAHC Press, 2001), p. 76.

Questions to be Addressed

1. What does it mean to bless my child?
2. How can parent-child bonds be strengthened with a blessing?

Evidence of Understanding

- Participants will discuss how *Birkat Y'ladim* fosters the building of spiritual connections and bonds between parent and child.
- Participants will recite *Birkat Y'ladim,* the blessing over children.

Session Overview

- Set Induction (10 minutes)
- Parent-Child Relationship Sentence Completion (40–45 minutes)
- *Birkat Y'ladim* Teaching (10-15 minutes)
- Small Group Discussion (10 minutes)
- Learning the Blessings (10 minutes)
- Conclusion (10 minutes)

Materials Needed

- Photocopies of handouts (pages 86–90)
- Pencils or pens

SESSION PLAN

Set Induction (10 minutes)

1. Share this text from the biblical book of Malachi with the session participants:

    > Lo, I will send the prophet Elijah to you before the coming of the great and awesome day of *Adonai.* He shall turn the hearts of the parents to their children and the hearts of the children to their parents. (Malachi 3:23–24)

2. Explain to the participants that the prophet Malachi ("my messenger" in Hebrew) was one of the later Hebrew prophets. His writings are placed in the middle of the fifth century before the common era.

He denounced what he believed was great corruption within the Jewish leadership and a high degree of immorality among the people.[2] The great and awesome day that this verse refers to is the messianic era, when peace and tranquility will reign over the earth. Elijah will come before that day, to let us know of its arrival.

3. Discuss the following questions:

   - What do you think it means to "turn the hearts of the parents to their children and the hearts of the children to their parents"?
   - Why do you think the messianic era will include turning the hearts of parents to their children and the hearts of children to their parents?
   - What does the biblical author seem to know about parent-child relationships?

Parent-Child Relationship Sentence Completion (40–45 minutes)

1. In this exercise parents have the opportunity to think and talk about how they communicate with their children. Arrange for the participants to be seated in circles of eight to ten participants each. Distribute copies of the handouts on pages 86–90. Appoint or ask for a volunteer to function as a facilitator in each group and instruct that individual to help the participants move through the activity. Ask participants to complete the open-ended sentences on page 86. As the participants complete each sentence, they should share their response to that sentence with the group before proceeding to the next sentence. Allow about 10 minutes for the sentence completions and about 30 minutes for the group discussion. The facilitator's role is to keep track of the time and to ensure that all the participants have the opportunity to respond.

2. Bring the whole group back together and invite discussion about the following questions:

   - Is it more important to a child's growth and development to reprimand or to praise? Which do you think parents do more of? Why?
   - How do our words affect our children? How do our children know what we are thinking and feeling about them?
   - In what ways can the content and tone of our messages affect how we communicate and connect with our children?

Birkat Y'ladim Teaching (10–15 minutes)

This segment of the session requires that the material that follows be presented to the whole group. The session leader can do this or you may want to ask a volunteer to read the text to the group.

The level of communication between parent and child may have its ups and downs during any given week. In Judaism there is a time set aside each week for parents to connect in a positive and

[2]Ronald H. Isaacs, *Messengers of God: A Jewish Prophet's Who's Who* (Northvale, N.J.: Jason Aronson, Inc., 1998), pp. 197–198.

loving way with their children. This custom is called *Birkat Y'ladim*—the blessing of children, which is recited right after the lighting and blessing of the Shabbat or holiday candles.

Birkat Y'ladim is an opportunity to emphasize an often overlooked dimension of the parent-child relationship. In the moment that we use to separate ourselves from the daily struggles and tensions of our workaday world to enter a Sabbath or holiday sanctuary of peace, we turn toward our children. As we bless them in the way that Jewish parents have been blessing their children throughout the centuries, we create a precious moment of connection and appreciation that hopefully opens the way to more caring communication between parent and child.

The custom of blessing children originated in the Bible. On his deathbed, Jacob called for his sons to surround his bed and be individually blessed (Genesis 49:1). He also chose to bless the sons of Joseph, Ephraim, and Menasheh (Genesis 48:12–20). Ephraim and Menasheh were the children of Joseph and his Egyptian-born wife, Osnath.

In the blessing for a son, the parent asks that his/her son be like Ephraim and Menasheh, the sons of Joseph. Ephraim and Menasheh demonstrated commitment to their heritage by maintaining their Jewishness despite the hostility and temptation of Egyptian culture.[3] Many Jewish parents today see this as a message we would like to impart to our children.

In the blessing for a daughter, the parent asks that his/her daughter be like Sarah, Rebekah, Leah, and Rachel. These women were the founding mothers of the Jewish people, but each in her own right had special and unique qualities. The biblical descriptions of the matriarchs give us insight into their characters.

Sarah, the wife of Abraham, is beautiful (Genesis 12:11) and she has a sense of humor (Genesis 18:12, 21:6). Rebekah, the wife of Isaac, shows hospitality to strangers and is kind to animals (Genesis 24:14–20). Both Leah and Rachel remain steadfastly loyal to Jacob in his quarrel with their father, Laban (Genesis 31:14–16). Leah was also strong-willed, for she chose to fight for Jacob's affection (Genesis 29:30–36). Wanting very much to have children, Rachel focused on that goal until she was successful (Genesis 30).

This blessing is followed by the Priestly Benediction, which comes from the Bible and is found in Numbers 6:24-26. This blessing asks God to bless and protect our children.

Small Group Discussion (10 minutes)

Divide the group into small groups of two or three people each. Ask them to respond to the following questions (page 87):

- The word *mitzvah* is translated as "commandment" but can also be understood as "sacred obligation." How might blessing your child(ren) be a sacred obligation?
- Would blessing your child create a spiritual bond or would it be a barrier? Share and explain.
- Based on what you have learned about Sarah, Rebekah, Leah, and Rachel, and Ephraim and Menasheh, are these meaningful role models for our daughters and sons? Explain.

---

[3]Nosson Scherman, ed., *Tanach: The Stone Edition* (2nd ed.) (Brooklyn, N.Y.: Mesorah Publications, Ltd., 1998), p. 126.

Learning the Blessings (10 minutes)

1. Bring the group together as a whole.
2. Ask participants to look at *Birkat Y'ladim* on page 88.
3. Read each blessing once, and then have participants recite it slowly with you.
4. As a group, repeat the saying of the blessings, slowly, three more times.
5. If time permits, you may want to ask the participants to practice one or two more times with a partner.
6. Ask the group to reflect upon the following questions:
    - Describe what benefits you and your family might derive from this observance.
    - What might be challenging for you to bring this observance into your home?

Conclusion (10 minutes)

1. Review Suggestions for Introducing *Birkat Y'ladim* to Your Family (page 89) as a group and invite discussion and questions.
2. Conclude by asking the participants to turn to a partner and to recite the Priestly Benediction, in Hebrew or in English, to each other. An alternative might be to say the Priestly Benediction as a group, intended for one another.
3. Review the Recommended Reading list (page 90) with participants before ending the session.

Parent-Child Relationship Sentence Completion

Complete the sentences.

- My greatest pleasure raising my child is

  ____.

- My child knows what my greatest pleasure is because

  ____.

- I am so happy when my child

  ____.

- My child knows when I am happy with him/her because

  ____.

- I am angry/upset with my child when

  ____.

- My child knows when I am upset with him/her because

  ____.

- I feel great pride when my child

  ____.

- My child knows when I feel pride in him/her because I

  ____.

Small Group Discussion Questions

1. The word מִצְוָה *mitzvah* is translated as "commandment" but can also be understood as "sacred obligation." How might blessing your child(ren) be a sacred obligation?

2. Would blessing your child create a spiritual bond or would it be a barrier? Share and explain.

3. Based on what you have learned about Sarah, Rebekah, Leah, and Rachel, and Ephraim and Menasheh, are these meaningful role models for our daughters and sons? Explain.

Birkat Y'ladim
Blessing the Children

FOR A BOY

Y'simcha Elohim k'Efrayim vechi-M'nasheh.

יְשִׂמְךָ אֱלֹהִים
כְּאֶפְרַיִם וְכִמְנַשֶּׁה.

May God inspire you to live in the tradition of Ephraim and Menasheh, who carried forward the life of our people.

FOR A GIRL

Y'simeich Elohim k'Sarah, Rivkah, Leah, v'Rachel

יְשִׂמֵךְ אֱלֹהִים כְּשָׂרָה,
רִבְקָה, לֵאָה וְרָחֵל.

May God inspire you to live in the tradition of Sarah, Rebekah, Leah, and Rachel, who carried forward the life of our people.

FOR BOTH

Y'varehch'cha Adonai v'yishm'rehcha.
Yaeir Adonai panav eilehcha
vichunehka.
Yisa Adonai panav eilehcha
v'yaseim l'cha shalom.

יְבָרֶכְךָ יְיָ וְיִשְׁמְרֶךָ.
יָאֵר יְיָ פָּנָיו אֵלֶיךָ
וִיחֻנֶּךָּ.
יִשָּׂא יְיָ פָּנָיו אֵלֶיךָ
וְיָשֵׂם לְךָ שָׁלוֹם.

May God bless you and keep you. May God look kindly upon you, and be gracious to you. May God reach out to you in tenderness, and give you peace.

Suggestions for Introducing *Birkat Y'ladim* to Your Family

- Share with your children what you learned about *Birkat Y'ladim* at this workshop.
- Talk with your children about incorporating this blessing into your Shabbat and holiday celebrations.
- Acknowledge that if this is something that your family has never done, it may feel odd or uncomfortable at first.
- Hold an open family discussion, sharing information you learned in this session.
- Encourage each family member to share thoughts and feelings about this possible addition to your family's ritual observances.
- When and if you choose to do this with your children, remind them that it is something new for the whole family but that you would like them to be willing to give it a place within family celebrations.
- Take some quiet time to compose your own special thoughts and wishes for your child that you would add to the traditional blessings or to replace the traditional blessings.
- Children may also want the opportunity to bless parents; encourage them to do this if they so desire.

Recommended Reading

A Gift of Prayer. New York: Women of Reform Judaism / UAHC Press, 2001 (see Blessing the Children, p. 33).

Perelson, Ruth. *An Invitation to Shabbat.* New York: UAHC Press, 1997.

Stern, Chaim, ed. *On the Doorposts of Your House: Prayers and Ceremonies for the Jewish Home*. New York: Central Conference of American Rabbis, 1994.

Avodah Session 3
Making the Connection: The Power of Jewish Ritual

Introduction

In this session, participants will discuss the meaning and purpose of ritual as a way of enriching their Jewish family life. Some leading psychologists and family therapists believe that the need to introduce or maintain rituals in family life is greater today than ever before. According to Dr. Ron Taffel, "Given all the stresses and strains of modern life . . . both the smallest expectable everyday routine and the largest, most significant rituals represent major quality time. . . . The bigger rituals—religious rites and/or holidays—are equally important today. In a world where it's so hard to connect, these occasions may be some of the only times you're actually together and can forge greater connections. Little kids obviously love these special times, but don't underestimate how much older kids—even when they object to them—still need to partake in meaningful rituals."[1]

In addition to considering the value of traditional rituals, participants will explore how creating *minhagim* —customs surrounding rituals—can personalize these acts and invest them with special meaning for each family. Finally, participants will consider ways in which they could begin adding to or enhancing the Jewish rituals they do or can do as a family.

Because this session deals with specific topics of Jewish observance, it would be preferable to select as the facilitator someone who is knowledgeable in this area and who can comfortably distinguish between prescribed ritual and *minhag*, since this understanding will be a factor in the session.

Enduring Understanding

Nurturing a strong Jewish identity requires the active participation of parents in their children's Jewish living and learning experiences.

Essential Questions

1. Who am I as a Jewish parent and a Jewish role model?

2. How does one establish a sacred relationship between parent and child?

---

[1]Ron Taffel with Melinda Blau, *Parenting by Heart: How to Be in Charge, Stay Connected, and Instill Your Values, When It Feels Like You've Got Only 15 Minutes a Day* (Reading, Mass.: Perseus Books, 1991), pp. 136–137.

3. What makes a meaningful Jewish life?

4. What does it mean to be a Jewish family?

Questions to Be Addressed

1. What is ritual?

2. What is a *minhag* (custom)?

3. How can ritual observance help connect an individual and a family to Judaism?

4. How does one create meaningful *minhagim* (customs) to accompany Jewish rituals?

Evidence of Understanding

- Participants will apply what they have learned about ritual and *minhag* to a given scenario.

- Participants discuss how to create family *minhagim* to personalize existing Jewish rituals or to create new ones.

Session Overview

- Set Induction (10 minutes)

- The Function of Ritual (20–25 minutes)

- *Minhag* as Enrichment (25–30 minutes)

- Conclusion (10–15 minutes)

Materials Needed

- Chalkboard and chalk or flip chart and markers

- Three posters labeled as per instructions on page 93

- Post-it notes

- Pens

- Photocopies of texts and handouts (page 95–102)

SESSION PLAN

Set Induction (10 minutes)

In this Set Induction, participants will explore the definition of ritual in terms of personal behaviors and ritual observance.

1. Prior to the session, write the Random House dictionary definition of *ritual* on the board or flip chart: A ritual is an established or prescribed procedure for a religious or other rite.

2. Discuss the following questions:

   - Can you think of any secular rituals that you or others may do? (*Leaving a tooth under a pillow for the tooth fairy, having special observances for family birthdays, eating dinner together as a family, kissing children goodnight.)* Who determines what those rituals will be? *(People, either individually or collectively.)*

   - Can you give examples of any religious rituals that you personally do or are aware of? *(Lighting Shabbat or holiday candles, saying* Kaddish *for a deceased relative, saying the* Sh'ma, *etc.)* Who determines what these rituals are? *(God, Jewish tradition, our ancestors, Jewish law, etc.)*

   Draw the distinction between the two types of ritual: secular rituals are those created by the individual and generally affect only the individual. Jewish rituals are connected to the community and in some way to God, and enable us to experience a larger sense of belonging.

3. Explain to the participants that in this session they will be exploring how Jewish rituals can help their family members experience a deeper sense of purpose and feel more connected to each other and to the Jewish community. Tell the participants that they will also have an opportunity to identify new ways of enacting rituals that will be enriching for them.

The Function of Ritual (20–25 minutes)

1. Prior to the session, create and hang three large posters. Write one of the following statements on each poster:

   Poster 1

   Jewish ritual is an anchor when _______________.

   Poster 2

   Jewish ritual is a safety net when ________________.

   Poster 3

   Jewish ritual is a springboard when _______________.

2. Distribute the handouts on pages 95–102 and invite a volunteer to read the following text (on page 95) to the group:

   Lighting Shabbat candles and participating in a Passover seder are some examples of Jewish ritual. Rituals give structure and meaning to life. The observance of ritual plays a significant role in creating a meaningful Jewish life. Life cycle ceremonies, the celebration of holidays, and the performance of mitzvot establish powerful historic and religious connections for us and our children. Rituals can serve different purposes. Ritual can anchor us to tradition, ritual can provide answers and serve as a safety net in times of uncertainty or distress, and ritual can encourage us to take new steps, serving as a springboard signaling a move forward in our lives.

3. Distribute to each participant a pen and three Post-it notes. Direct the participants to write a response to each of the statements on the posters on the Post-it notes. Ask them to place the Post-it notes on the appropriate posters. Then discuss the following questions (page 95):

- When has ritual served as an anchor connecting you to Jewish tradition?
- When has ritual served as a safety net providing answers for you?
- When has ritual been a springboard encouraging you to take new steps in your life?
- Have events ever changed or transformed for you because there was a ritual involved?
- How were you affected by those rituals?

Minhag as Enrichment (25–30 minutes)

In this activity, participants will examine the difference between ritual and *minhag*. They will read a story about a family observing Chanukah then consider as a group ways in which the family could develop *minhagim* that would enrich its celebration.

1. Explain to the participants that *minhag* (plural, *minhagim*) is the Hebrew word for "custom." A *minhag* develops to enhance and expand the observance of Jewish rituals. Suggest that they think of a Jewish ritual as a commanded Jewish behavior and a *minhag* as an optional observance.
2. Ask a volunteer to read the scenario on page 96 aloud for the group.
3. Divide the participants into small groups of five to seven people and ask them to discuss the following:
   - How could the Harris family enhance and expand the ritual moment of lighting the Chanukah candles? What *minhagim* might the Harris family adopt that would add meaning and depth to the lighting of the Chanukah candles? Think about ways for them to address the custom of doing no work during the half-hour during which the candles are burning.
   - What ritual moments have you and your family observed that also have special customs attached?
4. Bring the group together as a whole and review the Examples of *Minhagim* found on page 97. Ask participants to work in pairs, reading the examples and noting any questions they may have.
5. Come back together as a whole group to review and answer questions that may arise from the reading.

Conclusion (10–15 minutes)

1. Ask participants to turn to Our Jewish Family Observance Planner on page 98. Go through the points one at a time and ask participants these questions after each one: Is this something you think your family would like to try? What help do you need to get started? Note significant comments on the board or flip chart.
2. If participants indicate a need for additional study, suggest to them any adult education programs your synagogue offers that may address the identified needs.
3. Review Some Examples of Rituals and *Minhagim* Created by Today's Jewish Families on page 102 to give participants an idea of the types of observances their families can create.
4. Review the bibliography, Resources on Jewish Ritual Observance and Parenting, on pages 99–102. If the temple library has any of these books in its collection, have them out and available for participants to peruse or borrow.

Exploring Ritual

Lighting Shabbat candles and participating in a Passover seder are some examples of Jewish ritual. Rituals give structure and meaning to life. The observance of ritual plays a significant role in creating a meaningful Jewish life. Life cycle ceremonies, the celebration of holidays, and the performance of mitzvot establish powerful historic and religious connections for us and our children. Rituals can serve different purposes. Ritual can anchor us to tradition, ritual can provide answers and serve as a safety net in times of uncertainty or distress, and ritual can encourage us to take new steps, serving as a springboard signaling a move forward in our lives.

Discussion Questions

1. When has ritual served as an anchor connecting you to Jewish tradition?
2. When has ritual served as a safety net providing answers for you?
3. When has ritual been a springboard encouraging you to take new steps in your life?
4. Have events ever changed or transformed for you because there was a ritual involved?
5. How were you affected by those rituals?

Scenario

The Harris family really enjoys the holiday of Chanukah. They have established the following customs and rituals for its observance: Before lighting candles, Mr. Harris and his children set up the Chanukah menorahs on the dining room table with the appropriate number of candles. Then the whole family gathers around the table. Mrs. Harris lights a match and kindles the *shamash*—the tall helper candle. Each family member then holds out his or her *shamash* to be lit. Next the whole family sings the blessings together as they kindle the Chanukah lights. The family then sings several Chanukah songs from song sheets they have put together. Afterwards each family member receives a gift to open. At that point the family adjourns to the kitchen to have dinner. The candles are left to burn down. Mrs. Harris has expressed some dissatisfaction with just leaving the candles. She would like to have something else happen, though she is unsure what she would like the family to do.

- How could the Harris family enhance and expand the ritual moment of lighting the Chanukah candles? What *minhagim* might the Harris family adopt that would add meaning and depth to the lighting of the Chanukah candles? Think about ways for them to address the custom of doing no work during the half-hour during which the candles are burning.

- What ritual moments have you and your family observed that also have special customs attached?

Examples of *Minhagim*

- Saying the blessing over the Torah reading is a Jewish ritual. It is a Sephardic *minhag* that when a parent is called for an *aliyah*—the honor of reciting the blessing over the Torah reading—the children stand up in the congregation and remain standing until the parent is off the *bimah* (the raised platform from where the service is led and the Torah is read) as a sign of respecting one's parent.

- Reciting the *Sh'ma* at bedtime is a Jewish ritual. What parents do with their children to accompany that ritual are particular family *minhagim.* One may read a child stories, sing a special song, or say special good-night words. There may be a particular toy or blanket that accompanies the child to bed.

- Preparing a Shabbat meal and reciting the blessings over the candles, wine, and challah before eating are Jewish rituals. There is a *minhag* of giving *tzedakah*—a donation of money (usually this is done by placing coins in a special container called a *tzedakah* box)—before lighting the candles. Eventually this money is donated to a cause or organization that the family chooses.

- During the course of the Jewish year many holidays are celebrated. Certain foods have become associated with particular holidays. Eating hamentashen on Purim, having a round challah on Rosh Hashanah, enjoying latkes on Chanukah if you are of Eastern European descent or *sufganiyot* (jelly doughnuts) if you follow the Israeli tradition, and preparing blintzes on Shavuot are all examples of *minhagim* around food items. On Passover there are many ritual foods, and Jewish laws evolved that put particular boundaries on the types of food that are to be eaten. By Jewish law we are not to consume anything that is leavened. There are distinctive Ashkenazi (Eastern European) and Sephardic (Spanish-Middle Eastern) customs regarding Passover foods. For example, Sephardic Jews eat rice and a variety of beans that Ashkenazi Jews would not consume on Passover.

Our Jewish Family Observance Planner

	Not doing, but could try	Are doing, but could enrich
Celebrating Shabbat and holidays		
Light candles	☐	☐
Bless children	☐	☐
Make *Kiddush*	☐	☐
Say *HaMotzi* (blessing over the challah)	☐	☐
Eat a special meal	☐	☐
Say/sing *Birkat HaMazon* (grace after meals)	☐	☐
Build a sukkah	☐	☐
Eat in a sukkah	☐	☐
Light the menorah and observe Chanukah	☐	☐
Fast on Yom Kippur	☐	☐
Celebrate Purim		
Hear the megillah	☐	☐
Eat, drink, and be merry!	☐	☐
Give money to the poor	☐	☐
Affix a mezuzah	☐	☐
Observe Passover		
Have/attend a seder	☐	☐
Clean the house so it's *chameitz*-free	☐	☐
Recite the *Sh'ma*		
at bedtime	☐	☐
in the morning	☐	☐
Other thoughts:	☐	☐

Resources on Jewish Ritual Observance and Parenting

Abramowitz, Yosef I., and Susan Silverman. *Jewish Family and Life: Traditions, Holidays, and Values for Today's Parents and Children.* New York: Golden Books, 1997. Hands-on Jewish activities based in tradition with modern innovation; touches many aspects of Jewish family life.

Adelman, Penina V., and Beth Haber. *Miriam's Well: Rituals for Jewish Women Around the Year.* 10th anniversary ed. New York: Biblio Press, 1996. Collection of creative women's rituals for life cycle and other celebrations.

Cardin, Nina Beth. *The Tapestry of Jewish Time: A Spiritual Guide to the Holidays and Life Cycle Events.* Springfield, N.J.: Behrman House, Inc., 2000. Guide to celebrating Jewish holidays, Shabbat, and life cycle rituals, integrating traditional and contemporary practices, texts, and stories.

Cardozo, Arlene Rossen. *Jewish Family Celebrations: The Sabbath, Festivals, and Ceremonies.* 2d ed. New York: St. Martin's Press, 1996. Guide to celebrating Jewish holidays, Shabbat, and life cycle rituals.

Danan, Julie Hilton. *The Jewish Parents' Almanac.* Northvale, N.J.: Jason Aronson, Inc., 1994. Comprehensive guide to Jewish parenting, family rituals, and celebrations.

Diamant, Anita, and Howard Cooper. *Living a Jewish Life: Jewish Traditions, Customs and Values for Today's Families.* New York: HarperCollins Publishers, 1996. Presents an overview of Jewish rituals for the family.

Diamant, Anita, and Karen Kushner. *How to Be a Jewish Parent: A Practical Handbook for Family Life.* New York: Schocken Books, Inc., 2000. Comprehensive guide to Jewish parenting and all that it entails.

Dosick, Wayne. *Living Judaism: The Complete Guide to Jewish Belief, Tradition and Practice.* San Francisco: HarperSanFrancisco, 1998. Informative guide to Jewish beliefs, traditions, holidays, worship, and life cycle.

Frishman, Elyse D. *Blessings for the Table.* New York: Central Conference of American Rabbis, 2000. Adapted from *On The Doorposts of Your House.* Contains readings, songs, and services for holidays and weddings.

Fuchs-Kreimer, Nancy. *Parenting as a Spiritual Journey: Deepening Ordinary and Extraordinary Events into Sacred Occasions.* Woodstock, Vt.: Jewish Lights Publishing, 1996. Includes descriptions of rituals and inspiring ideas from Jewish text sources, as well as other religious traditions.

Geffen, Rela M., ed. *Celebration and Renewal: Rites of Passage in Judaism.* Philadelphia: Jewish Publication Society, 1993. Essays about the Jewish life cycle.

Grishaver, Joel Lurie. *40 Things You Can Do to Save the Jewish People.* Los Angeles: Alef Design Group, 2000. "Some really practical ideas for parents who want to raise 'good enough' Jewish kids."

Isaacs, Ronald H., and Kerry M. Olitzky. *The Second How-To Handbook for Jewish Living.* Hoboken, N.J.: KTAV Publishing House, Inc., 1996. Step-by-step explanation of many Jewish rituals.

Levine, Elizabeth Resnick, ed. *A Ceremonies Sampler: New Rites, Celebrations, and Observances of Jewish Women.* San Diego: Woman's Institute for Continuing Jewish Education, 1991. Collection of contemporary rituals for Jewish women.

Maslin, Simeon J., ed. *Gates of Mitzvah: A Guide to the Jewish Life Cycle.* New York: Central Conference of American Rabbis, 1986. Reform Judaism's statement about mitzvot that Jews should do in observing life cycle events.

Orenstein, Rabbi Debra, ed. *Lifecycles: Jewish Women on Life Passages and Personal Milestones,* vol. 1. Woodstock, Vt.: Jewish Lights Publishing, 1994. Collection of essays and rituals by Jewish women pertaining to life cycle, from birth through death.

Robinson, George. *Essential Judaism: A Complete Guide to Beliefs, Customs, and Rituals.* New York: Pocket Books, 2000.

Siegel, Richard, Michael Strassfeld, and Sharon Strassfeld. *The First Jewish Catalog.* Philadelphia: Jewish Publication Society, 1973. A how-to guide to Judaism, on life cycle and ritual observances.

Stern, Chaim, ed. *On the Doorposts of Your House: Prayers and Ceremonies for the Jewish Home.* New York: Central Conference of American Rabbis, 1995. Reform Judaism's prayers and ceremonies for the home.

Washofsky, Mark. *Jewish Living: A Guide to Contemporary Reform Practice.* New York: UAHC Press, 2001. Reform Jewish religious practice, holidays, and life cycle observances.

Some Examples of Rituals and *Minhagim* Created by Today's Jewish Families

- At the Shabbat dinner table, ask each person to take a turn and share "what was the sweetest thing" that happened to him or her that week.
- At the Passover seder, set out a beautiful cup (often filled with water) to represent Miriam and the legend of the well.
- Say a special blessing for a daughter upon reaching puberty.
- Have special "dress up" pajamas for very young children that are worn to the dinner table only on Shabbat or holidays.

Avodah Session 4
One Hundred Blessings Every Day

INTRODUCTION

"The Rabbis tell us that we should attempt to say one hundred blessings a day," writes Rabbi Nina Beth Cardin. "By encouraging us to do so, they are teaching us a profound lesson. One hundred times a day we should be alert to the wonders of life around us."[1] Reciting a blessing brings a moment of the sacred into the everyday. Blessings demonstrate our gratitude and appreciation of our world and all that is good in it. Surely this is a perspective that parents desire their children to have. A child's view of the world often acknowledges the wonder of the universe; blessings provide a Jewish context. This session invites parents to reflect on the role of blessing in their own lives and to reach a deeper understanding of Jewish blessings. In this session, we will explore the origin of the tradition of reciting blessings and give parents the tools to begin incorporating this tradition into their family's lives.

In these sessions, we are frequently asking parents to learn about and try Jewish practices that are new to them. This session is a wonderful opportunity for the presenter to model this kind of learning. During the week before the session, try incorporating the habit of saying a new blessing in your day-to-day life. Try to be conscious of how this new behavior affects you, and share it with the participants at the beginning of the session. What was challenging? What was enlightening? Will you continue to incorporate this blessing, and how? What kinds of supports or resources would help you to adopt this new habit?

ENDURING UNDERSTANDING

Nurturing a strong Jewish identity requires the active participation of parents in their children's Jewish living and learning experiences.

ESSENTIAL QUESTIONS

1. Who am I as a Jewish parent and a Jewish role model?
2. How does one establish a sacred relationship between parent and child?
3. What makes a meaningful Jewish life?
4. What does it mean to be a Jewish family?

---

[1]Nina Beth Cardin, "Blessings Throughout the Day," in *The Rituals and Practices of a Jewish Life*, ed. Kerry M. Olitzky and Daniel Judson (Woodstock, Vt.: Jewish Lights Publishing, 2002), p. 131.

Questions to Be Addressed

1. What are the components of a Jewish blessing?
2. How can blessings affect my family's life?
3. What are my goals and plans for incorporating blessings into my life and my family's life?

Evidence of Understanding

- Participants will reflect on the benefits and challenges of incorporating more blessings into their family lives.
- Participants will articulate goals and a plan for incorporating *b'rachot* (blessings) into their family lives.

Session Overview

- Set Induction (15–20 minutes)
- Investigating *B'rachot* (20 minutes)
- Planning to Incorporate *B'rachot* (20–30 minutes)
- Conclusion (10–15 minutes)

Materials Needed

- Daily Blessings Card from the URJ Press (**www.urjpress.com** or 888-489-8242)
- Chalkboard and chalk or flip chart and markers
- Photocopies of handouts (pages 108–110)

SESSION PLAN

Set Induction (15–20 minutes)

1. Write the following words in Hebrew, transliteration, and English on the board or flip chart:

   בָּרוּךְ אַתָּה יְיָ אֱלֹהֵינוּ מֶלֶךְ הָעוֹלָם

   Baruch atah Adonai Eloheinu melech haolam . . .

   Blessed are You, *Adonai* our God, Ruler of the universe . . .

2. Ask the group to brainstorm blessings that they know, prayers that begin with these six words. (Possible answers include: *blessing over wine, blessing over bread, blessing over holiday candles, Shehecheyanu, blessings from the synagogue service such as morning blessings.*)

3. Ask the group when they generally say blessings as a family: at a meal or holiday celebration, in synagogue, or just in the course of their day-to-day lives. Ask any individual parents who may have special rituals within their families to share these with the group. Would these special rituals be enhanced by blessings? Ask participants to share their own ideas about why they might want to incorporate blessings in their daily lives. How can offering a blessing change a moment? At this point, the facilitator may want to share a story about how experimenting with adding a new blessing affected moments in his or her life the past week.

4. Distribute the handouts on pages 108–110 and read One Hundred Blessings Every Day on page 110. Ask participants to share any feelings they have about how saying blessings might positively affect family life.

5. Ask the participants to share those things that challenge them about incorporating blessings and record them on the board. Do they know what blessings to say? Are they afraid of having overly zealous children who are always invoking God's name? Do the blessings have meaning, or are they rote? Address some concerns by explaining that this session is designed to explain some of the history and meaning behind the tradition of saying *b'rachot* (blessings) as to well as provide some resources and support that will allow parents to feel confident in teaching their children about saying *b'rachot.*

INVESTIGATING *B'RACHOT* (20 MINUTES)

1. Ask participants to take a second look at the six-word *b'rachah* formula on the board. Draw a line after the second word and after the fourth word. Ask the participants to look at each segment of the formula and share ideas about what the design of the prayer can teach us about the purpose of prayer. After participants share their thoughts, point out that in six words, this formula takes the person praying from the individual (You) to the community (our God), to the entire world (the universe). With the proper intention and understanding, reciting *b'rachot* can affect the way we perceive ourselves and the world.

2. Share the following quote:

   > According to the Bible, it is sacrilegious to appropriate objects from the temple for personal use. If the whole world is the Lord's temple, I might fear that all is off limits. Our rabbis tell me otherwise. By uttering a blessing, I become a denizen of God's temple. Within the precincts of the temple, we may partake of all temple objects. If my mind and my lips are in the right place, nothing is off limits.[2]

   Explain that essentially, prayer replaced the Temple service when the Temple was destroyed. Offering blessings every day reassures us that God did not disappear from the world with the destruction of the Temple; rather, the whole world is God's Temple. This shift in perspective was an ingenious interpretation of the Rabbis that allowed Judaism to survive the terrible blow of the destruction of the Temple and to grow into and thrive as the Judaism we practice today.

3. Discuss the following in pairs or as a whole group: Some people note that the number 100 corresponds to the number of sockets that held together the structure of the ancient tabernacle. What is the significance of connecting individual prayers and the sockets that held together the tabernacle?

---

[2]Reuven Kimelman, "The Blessings of Prayerobics," *B'nai Brith International Jewish Monthly,* 1986.

Planning to Incorporate *B'rachot* (20–30 minutes)

1. Explain to the group: Now that we have talked about the significance of saying *b'rachot* and some of the history behind the tradition, we are going to make concrete plans for incorporating *b'rachot* into our lives. Ask for ideas from the group: Thinking back on the past day, week, or month, name some moments that could have been enhanced by the reciting of a blessing. As you record ideas on the board, record them in three columns, based on the following three categories:
   - בִּרְכוֹת הַנֶּהֱנִין *Birchot HaNehenin*: blessings of enjoyment. These are said before eating or when experiencing something connected to one of the five senses. Examples of this type of blessing are *HaMotzi* (the blessing over bread); the blessings for drinking wine, smelling spices, seeing lightning, shooting stars, or other natural phenomena; and the blessing for seeing a scholar.
   - בִּרְכוֹת הַמִּצְווֹת *Birchot HaMitzvot*: blessings recited before performing a commanded behavior. Examples of this type of blessing are for lighting Shabbat and holiday candles, blowing the shofar, and sitting in the sukkah.
   - בִּרְכוֹת הוֹדָיָה *Birchot Hodayah*: blessings that express our gratitude to God. The best examples of these blessings are those found in our prayer books in such blessings as the *Shehecheyanu* (for enabling us to reach this moment) and *Birchot HaShachar*—the morning blessings.
2. After you have generated some examples in each of the three columns, ask the group what they think the occasions in each column have in common, that is, what the name of the category might be. As the group comes to conclusions, write the three headings in Hebrew and English above each column.
3. Distribute the Daily Blessing Cards and review some of the blessings there. Choose blessings that relate to those occasions generated by the group on the chart. Ask participants to select one blessing they would like to begin to incorporate. Ask them which blessing they think might appeal to their families and how they will encourage their family members to recite it.
4. Review the Family Blessing Ideas sheet on page 108. You may want to have participants write their plan for incorporating the blessing they have chosen on the back of the sheet.

Conclusion (10–15 minutes)

One blessing not included on the Daily Blessings Card is the *Shehecheyanu*. This blessing can be said anytime something is done for the first time, or for the first time in a season, or just to express thanks for being able to experience a particular moment. Ask participants to look at the words to this prayer (page 109) and suggest that they recite it as a group to celebrate participating in a parent education session and making a plan to incorporate blessing into their family's lives. Ask participants for other reasons to say this prayer (meeting new people, learning something new, participating in a new program). Recite it together. Conclude by encouraging participants to share with each other how they are doing incorporating blessings when they see each other in the coming months.

Blessings included on the Daily Blessings Card, available from the URJ Press:

For Various Foods

- For bread
- For wine or grape juice

- For cereals and pastry
- For fruits that grow on trees
- For vegetables and fruits that grow in the soil
- For all other foods and liquids

For Life Moments

- For joyous occasions
- On hearing good tidings
- On hearing of a death
- On recovering from serious illness or upon escape from danger
- For courage

For Wonders of Nature

- On seeing the large-scale wonders of nature
- On seeing the small-scale wonders of nature
- On seeing a rainbow
- For flowers and herbs

For a Journey

- *Tefilat Haderech*

For Learning

- Before the study of Torah

For Social Action

- Before performing an act of *tzedek*/justice

Available by the dozen at **www.URJPress.com**, product #658752.

Family Blessing Ideas

Blessings Discussion

With your children, talk about the following topics related to blessings:

- What is a blessing?
- How do we identify blessings that are part of our lives?
- How can we find blessings in everyday life?
- How has Judaism included blessing as part of its tradition?

Birchot HaNehenin: Blessings of Enjoyment/Using Our Five Senses

- Ask your children to create illustrations of *Birchot HaNehenin*.
- Take a nature walk and look for opportunities to offer blessings over the sights and smells and tastes.
- Write key words of blessings on stickers and place them around the house (on the refrigerator, kitchen table, window, etc.) or on body parts (hands, eyes, nose, etc.) that are connected to the experience over which the blessing is said.

Family Book of Blessings: An Interactive Family Journal

Create a "Family Book of Blessings." In a scrapbook, record your family's ideas about the blessings that are part of your life. Include the blessing you would say over these moments as well as photos, stories, souvenirs, and other reminders of the blessings in your lives.

On the back of this page, write your plan for incorporating a new blessing into your family's life and how you hope it will affect your family's life.

Shehecheyanu

בָּרוּךְ אַתָּה יְיָ אֱלֹהֵינוּ מֶלֶךְ הָעוֹלָם, שֶׁהֶחֱיָנוּ וְקִיְּמָנוּ וְהִגִּיעָנוּ לַזְּמַן הַזֶּה.

Baruch atah Adonai, Eloheinu melech haolam shehecheyanu v'kiymanu v'higiyanu laz'man hazeh.

We praise You, Eternal God, Sovereign of the universe, for giving us life, for sustaining us, and for enabling us to reach this season.

One Hundred Blessings Every Day

The Rabbis tell us that we should attempt to say one hundred blessings a day. By encouraging us to do so, they are teaching us a profound lesson. One hundred times a day we should be alert to the wonders of life around us.

(RABBI NINA BETH CARDIN, "BLESSINGS THROUGHOUT THE DAY," IN *THE RITUALS AND PRACTICES OF A JEWISH LIFE,* ED. KERRY M. OLITZKY AND DANIEL JUDSON [WOODSTOCK, VT.: JEWISH LIGHTS PUBLISHING, 2002], P. 131)

Avodah Session 5
With These Words: God, Spirituality, Prayer, and Parenting

Introduction

Talking about God, spirituality, and prayer with children can make many parents uncomfortable. Finding the right words and how to express them are important Jewish parenting skills. This session seeks to empower the participants to develop a conversational comfort level on these subjects and to become aware of the resources available to help them talk about God, spirituality, and prayer with their children.

Enduring Understanding

Nurturing a strong Jewish identity requires the active participation of parents in their children's Jewish living and learning experiences.

Essential Questions

1. Who am I as a Jewish parent and a Jewish role model?
2. How does one establish a sacred relationship between parent and child?
3. What makes a meaningful Jewish life?
4. What does it mean to be a Jewish family?

Questions to Be Addressed

1. What resources on God, spirituality, and prayer are available for parents?
2. In what ways is Jewish prayer life-changing and life-enhancing?
3. How can I begin to talk about God, spirituality, and prayer with my children?

Evidence of Understanding

- Participants will complete the I Believe Prayer Is . . . worksheet.
- Participants will consider different views of prayer and God and will discuss their own reactions and beliefs with regard to these.
- Participants will ask questions and share personal thoughts, feelings, and insights about God, spirituality, and prayer.

Session Overview

- Set Induction (10 minutes)
- Reflection and Discussion (10–15 minutes)
- Small Group Text Study (45–50 minutes)
- Conclusion (10–15 minutes)

Materials Needed

- Photocopies of text and handouts (pages 114–119)
- Chalkboard and chalk or flip chart and markers
- Pens or pencils

SESSION PLAN

Set Induction (10 minutes)

Distribute the handouts on pages 114–119. Ask participants to read the I Believe Prayer Is . . . worksheet on page 114 and complete the questions by themselves. Inform them that these will not be shared with the group, but they will be reviewing their own answers later in the session.

Reflection and Discussion (10–15 minutes)

In this activity, participants will consider the impact of their own attitudes about prayer on their children.

1. Ask participants to turn to the Text Study sheet on page 115 and ask a volunteer to read the first text out loud to the group.
2. Pose the following questions for discussion:
   - What is your reaction to this quote? What do you think Rabbi Wolpe is trying to communicate to parents?
   - Do you agree that belief in God is important for children?
   - How do you think your assessment about your own beliefs and attitudes might affect the way you communicate with your child on this subject?

Small Group Text Study (45–50 minutes)

1. Ask the participants to arrange themselves into small study groups of two or three and to read the remaining texts on the Text Study sheets on pages 115–117. They should address/answer the questions that follow each text. Circulate among the groups to be sure they are moving through the texts and to answer any questions the participants may have.

2. Bring the small groups back together and invite the participants to share their thoughts and reactions to the study session. Point out to the participants that all the texts they studied were written by contemporary rabbis. Ask them their opinion about the diversity of viewpoints expressed.

Conclusion (10–15 minutes)

1. Have the participants turn back to the I Believe Prayer Is . . . sheet they completed earlier in the session and ask them if they would change any of their answers or add anything new based on today's session. Point out that much about our success in teaching our children depends on our own true feelings and beliefs, which the group had an opportunity to explore in the session.

2. Review the Reading Resource List on God, Spirituality, Prayer, and Parenting on pages 118–119 and explain that these are some of the many resources available to help parents advance their own thinking and communicate more clearly with their children about these topics.

I Believe Prayer Is . . .

Indicate which of the following answers reflect your personal feelings:

I believe prayer is . . .

. . . a way to stay connected to our people's past.

. . . a form of relaxation and/or personal meditation.

. . . an opportunity to thank God for the blessings in my life.

. . . a way to experience Judaism within my synagogue community.

. . . self-reflection that helps me grow and change.

Your own thoughts:

____

____

____

____

____

____

Text Study

Text 1

For a child to believe in God's concern is not an intellectual proposition or a philosophical decision. It is a way of trusting in the goodness of the world.

(DAVID J. WOLPE, *TEACHING YOUR CHILDREN ABOUT GOD: A MODERN JEWISH APPROACH* [NEW YORK: HARPER PERENNIAL, 1995], P. 7)

Text 2

Prayer invites God to let God's presence suffuse our spirits, to let God's will prevail in our lives. Prayer cannot bring water to parched fields, nor mend a broken bridge, nor rebuild a ruined city; but prayer can water an arid soul, mend a broken heart, and rebuild a weakened will.

(ADAPTED FROM *GATES OF PRAYER: THE NEW UNION PRAYER BOOK* [NEW YORK: CENTRAL CONFERENCE OF AMERICAN RABBIS, 1975], P. 152)

- According to this author, what is God's "role" in the world? What is ours?
- How might you explain this point of view to your child?

Text 3

The tension between power and powerlessness makes some parents want to feel part of something larger than themselves. One mother told me that when she first read the Bible as an adult with two young children, she couldn't get over how the characters sounded like the roster of her daughter's yuppie preschool—Sarah, Rebecca, Joshua. Of course, she realized it was the nursery school parents who were borrowing from the Bible, not the other way around! It occurred to her that in naming children, this very secular, post-modern generation was expressing its yearning for tradition. The sociologist Peter Berger speaks of religion as a "sacred canopy" under which the believer lives her life. Parents often find themselves reweaving their canopies, sometimes borrowing threads from afar, in order to create for their children—and themselves—a place to take shelter.

(NANCY FUCHS-KREIMER, *PARENTING AS A SPIRITUAL JOURNEY* [WOODSTOCK, VT.: JEWISH LIGHTS PUBLISHING, 1996], P. 11)

- What do you think the author means by "the tension between power and powerlessness"? Do you experience these two feelings as a parent? If so, under what circumstances?

- Some parents find that having their children attend Religious School and being a part of the synagogue community helps them create a "sacred canopy." Do you feel this way?

Text 4

The source of light may be so deeply hidden within us that we cannot see it, until we lose the faith that it exists at all. Then another, whose light may be more visible to us than our own, shines forth in such a way that our own light is called out of hiding. This other may be a lover, friend, or teacher; the communication may take the form of mountain, well, or bolt of lightning. In our opening to one another, our two lights meet, casting forth a new light. This light is surely brighter and more widely seen than was the sum of our two faint lights as they had existed before our meeting. And so the light grows. The creation of human community is the redeeming of sparks of holy light.

(ARTHUR GREEN, *SEEK MY FACE, SPEAK MY NAME: A CONTEMPORARY JEWISH THEOLOGY* [NORTHVALE, N.J.: JASON ARONSON, INC., 1994], P. 189)

- Has the spirituality of another person ever deeply affected your sense of the sacred? If so, can you describe the experience?

- In what ways do you now, or might you in the future, share your sense of the sacred with your family?

Text 5

Though we know much about God, we also know that God far transcends what we can know about God. We do not know why the good God permits the evils of this world but we trust God anyway. We do so out of gratitude and awe. Each day, rising up and lying down, if we can say the hundred blessings required of a Jew, we are reminded of God's continual gifts. Our observance teaches a piety of the ordinary, a hallowing of the many gifts we might otherwise arrogantly consider ours by right. This daily thanksgiving sets the context for facing the evils beyond our control or understanding; it enables many people to accept the unexplainable.

(EUGENE B. BOROWITZ, *RENEWING THE COVENANT: A THEOLOGY FOR THE POSTMODERN JEW* [PHILADELPHIA: THE JEWISH PUBLICATION SOCIETY, 1991], PP. 38–39)

- How, according to this author, can we trust in a God who allows evil to exist in the world?
- What do you think the author is saying about the value of belief? Do you agree?

Reading Resource List on God, Spirituality, Prayer, and Parenting

Abramowitz, Yosef I., and Susan Silverman. *Jewish Family and Life: Traditions, Holidays, and Values for Today's Parents and Children.* New York: Golden Books, 1997. (parents)

Abrams, Judith Z., and Dr. Steven A. Abrams. *Jewish Parenting: Rabbinic Insights.* Northvale, N.J.: Jason Aronson, Inc., 1994.

Bogot, Howard I., and Daniel B. Syme. *I Learn About God.* New York: UAHC Press, 1998. (parents and children)

Brichto, Mira Pollak. *The God Around Us: A Child's Garden of Prayer*, rev. ed. New York: UAHC Press, 1999. (parents and children)

_____. *The God Around Us: The Valley of Blessings*, vol. II. New York: UAHC Press, 2001. (parents and children)

Cone, Molly. *Hello, Hello, Are You There God?* New York: UAHC Press, 1999. (parents and children)

Diamant, Anita, with Karen Kushner. *How to Be a Jewish Parent: A Practical Handbook for Family Life.* New York: Schocken Books, Inc., 2000. (parents)

Dosick, Wayne. *Soul Judaism: Dancing with God into a New Era.* Woodstock, Vt.: Jewish Lights Publishing, 1999. (parents)

Ehrlich, Elizabeth. *Miriam's Kitchen: A Memoir.* New York: Penguin Books, 1997.

Fuchs-Kreimer, Nancy. *Parenting as a Spiritual Journey.* Woodstock, Vt.: Jewish Lights Publishing, 1996. (parents)

Gellman, Marc, and Thomas Hartman. *Where Does God Live? Questions and Answers for Parents and Children.* New York: Ballantine Books, 1996. (parents and children)

Goodman, Roberta Louis, and Sherry H. Blumberg. *Teaching About God and Spirituality: A Resource for Jewish Settings.* Denver: Alternatives in Religious Education, 2002. (parents)

Hilton Danan, Julie. *The Jewish Parents' Almanac.* Northvale, N.J.: Jason Aronson, Inc., 1993. (parents)

Kushner, Harold. *When Children Ask About God: A Guide for Parents Who Don't Always Have All the Answers.* New York: Schocken Books, Inc., 1995. (parents)

Kushner, Lawrence. *The Book of Miracles.* Woodstock, Vt.: Jewish Lights Publishing, 1987. (parents and children)

Kushner, Lawrence, and Karen Kushner. *Because Nothing Looks Like God.* Woodstock, Vt.: Jewish Lights Publishing, 2000. (parents and children)

_____. *Where Is God?* Woodstock, Vt.: Jewish Lights Publishing, 2000. (parents and young children)

_____. *How Does God Make Things Happen?* Woodstock, Vt.: Jewish Lights Publishing, 2001. (parents and young children)

Matlins, Stuart, M. ed. *The Jewish Lights Spirituality Handbook: A Guide to Understanding, Exploring, and Living a Spiritual Life.* Woodstock, Vt.: Jewish Lights Publishing, 2001. (parents)

Mogel, Wendy. *The Blessing of a Skinned Knee: Using Jewish Teachings to Raise Self-Reliant Children.* New York: Penguin Compass, 2001. (parents)

Musleah, Rahel, and Michael Klayman. *Sharing Blessings.* Woodstock, Vt.: Jewish Lights Publishing, 1997. (parents and children)

Olitzky, Kerry M., and Lori Forman. *Restful Reflections.* Woodstock, Vt.: Jewish Lights Publishing, 2001. (parents)

Olitzky, Kerry, and Ronald H. Isaacs. *Third How-To Handbook for Jewish Living.* Hoboken, N.J.: KTAV, 2002. (parents)

Sasso, Sandy Eisenberg. *God In Between.* Woodstock, Vt.: Jewish Lights Publishing, 1998. (parents and children)

_____ . *God Said Amen.* Woodstock, Vt.: Jewish Lights Publishing, 2000. (parents and children)

_____. *God's Paintbrush.* Woodstock, Vt.: Jewish Lights Publishing, 1993. (parents and children)

Sonsino, Rifat, and Daniel B. Syme. *Finding God: Selected Responses,* rev. ed. New York: UAHC Press, 2002. (parents)

Avodah Session 6
Thirteen Steps on the Path of Jewish Beliefs, Values, and Ethics

INTRODUCTION

The Jewish prayer book represents our deepest held beliefs, values, and ethics, based on teachings from the Torah. Rabbi Hayim Halevi Donin expresses it this way: "Jewish prayer is prayer that uses the idiom of the Hebrew Bible and reflects the Jewish soul. It is prayer that expresses the basic values of the Jewish people and affirms the central articles of Jewish faith."[1] According to the Mishnah, the *Amidah*, the central prayer of Jewish worship, must be said with complete *kavanah*, purposeful intention, even more so than the *Sh'ma,* because the *Amidah* epitomizes the Jewish people's longing for personal, communal, and national redemption and world peace.[2]

In this session, participants will examine the intermediate blessings of the *Amidah* to identify the enduring values of the Jewish people that are expressed in the prayer. They will make a connection between these blessings and their own lives, and they will create a model for explaining the blessings to their children. For additional background information, you may want to refer to *Avodah* Lessons 2 through 5 in the *CHAI Level 5 Curriculum Core*, which focus on the *Amidah*.

ENDURING UNDERSTANDING

Nurturing a strong Jewish identity requires the active participation of parents in their children's Jewish living and learning experiences.

ESSENTIAL QUESTIONS

1. Who am I as a Jewish parent and a Jewish role model?
2. How does one establish a sacred relationship between parent and child?
3. What makes a meaningful Jewish life?
4. What does it mean to be a Jewish family?

---

[1]From *To Pray as a Jew,* quoted in *A Treasury of Thoughts on Jewish Prayer,* ed. Sidney Greenberg (Northvale, N.J.: Jason Aronson, Inc., 1989), p. 165.
[2]Arnold S. Rosenberg, *Jewish Liturgy as a Spiritual System* (Northvale N.J.: Jason Aronson, Inc., 1997), pp. 74–75.

Questions to Be Addressed

1. What are the sources of Jewish values, beliefs, and ethics?
2. What values, beliefs, and ethics are contained in the thirteen intermediate petitionary prayers of the *Amidah*?
3. What influence do (can) the thirteen intermediate petitionary prayers have on our lives as Jews?
4. How can parents instill these Jewish values, beliefs, and ethics in their children?

Evidence of Understanding

- Participants will identify the sources of their Jewish values, beliefs, and ethics.
- Participants will discuss the Jewish values, beliefs, and ethics represented in the thirteen intermediate petitionary blessings of the *Amidah*.
- Participants will suggest ways that they can translate these prayers from words into actions for themselves and for their children.

Session Overview

- Set Induction (10–15 minutes)
- Overview of the *Amidah* (10 minutes)
- Exploring the Intermediate Blessings (30–35 minutes)
- Text Study (5–10 minutes)
- Teaching Our Children (20 minutes)
- Conclusion (5–10 minutes)

Materials Needed

- *Siddurim*—a prayer book for every one or two participants
- Photocopies of text and handouts (pages 126–131)
- Chalkboard and chalk or flip chart and markers

SESSION PLAN

Set Induction (10–15 minutes)

1. Prior to the session, write this text on a piece of flip chart paper, but do not post it yet:

Jewish prayer is prayer that uses the idiom of the Hebrew Bible and reflects the Jewish soul. It is prayer that expresses the basic values of the Jewish people and affirms the central articles of Jewish faith. (Rabbi Hayim Halevi Donin)[3]

2. Ask participants to identify one value, belief, or ethic they understand to be Jewish. Write these on the board or flip chart.

3. Next, ask the participants to identify where they think they learned the value, belief, or ethic they just named. Write these sources on the board, too.

4. Post the Rabbi Donin text and ask participants for their reactions to it, especially in light of the answers they gave to the preceding two questions.

Overview of the *Amidah* (10 minutes)

1. Distribute prayer books so that participants can follow along when you describe the *Amidah.*

2. Provide participants with the following overview, either by reading it aloud, asking a volunteer to read it aloud, or by distributing it and having different volunteers read assigned sections.

   The prayer book (*siddur*) contains many of the values, beliefs, and ethics of Judaism. We will be looking at a specific section of the worship service called the *Amidah.*

   The *Amidah* is comprised of three sections. The first section contains three introductory blessings (*b'rachot*) that focus on praising God. The second section contains thirteen petitionary blessings. Originally this section contained twelve blessings, but ultimately the twelfth blessing was divided into two, making a total of thirteen blessings in this section. These thirteen blessings are not said on Shabbat and holidays, for it is considered inappropriate to ask God to fulfill requests on those days. The last section of the *Amidah* also has three blessings. The first talks about the benefits of prayer, the second blessing is a prayer of thanksgiving and praise to God, and the last blessing is a prayer for peace. The total number of blessings is nineteen. These blessings can also be called prayers.

   This collection of nineteen blessings is known by any of the following three names: *Amidah, Sh'moneh Esreih,* or *HaT'filah.* The first, *Amidah,* means standing; this name was given to these blessings because they are said in a standing position. The second name for these blessings *Sh'moneh Esreih,* means eighteen; though technically inaccurate since there are now nineteen blessings, this name remained. Lastly, these blessings are known as *HaT'filah,* which translates as "the prayer," since this collection of blessings is considered the central core of the worship service.

   The focus of our session is the thirteen intermediate petitionary blessings of the *Amidah* and the values, beliefs, and ethics they represent.

[3]From *To Pray as a Jew,* quoted in *A Treasury of Thoughts on Jewish Prayer,* ed. Sidney Greenberg (Northvale, N.J.: Jason Aronson, Inc., 1989), p. 165.

Exploring the Intermediate Blessings (30–35 minutes)

1. Divide the participants into groups of three; if necessary make one group of four. Distribute copies of the handouts on pages 126–131.

2. Ask the participants to read through the English translations of the thirteen intermediate blessings of the *Amidah* on pages 126–129, rotating the reading among the members of the triad. Tell them to take notes on the subject of each of these blessings.

3. When they are done, have pairs of triads join together to make groups of six. Ask them to discuss the first two questions on page 130:
   - What belief, value, or ethic is found in each of these blessings?
   - How do you think saying the blessings might inspire positive action on your part? How might you translate the hopes expressed in blessings into realities?

4. In their present groups of six, ask the participants to read through the thirteen blessings again and find words that are the opposites of each other (e.g., affliction and healing, transgression and repentance, evil and righteousness). Using these word pairs state a problem with the negative word and then create a solution with its opposite. For example:

   When I see **evil** like _______ I can work for **righteousness** by ________________.

   When I **transgress** by _______ I can **repent** by ______________________.

   When I see **affliction** like _____________ I can **heal** by ________________________ .

   Also ask the participants to respond to the following question and to prepare a statement to share with the other groups: What kind of Jewish life do you think is envisioned in these blessings?

5. Reassemble into one large group and have the groups of six share the statements about the kind of Jewish life envisioned in the intermediate blessings of the *Amidah.*

Text Study (5–10 minutes)

1. Read the following text to the participants, which can be found on page 131:

   > Rabbi Daniel Landes has written, "Each of the middle petitionary blessings has ethical consequences for us who pray it. Since we ask God to do these things, it must be in God's nature to do them; since we are made in God's image, it must be our nature also to do them, when we act in a godly way. The middle blessings are, therefore, more than requests we make of God. They are equally a catalogue of our own responsibilities."[4]

2. Discuss the following questions:
   - In what ways are these thirteen blessings of the *Amidah* building blocks for an ethical, values-rich Jewish life?
   - What is our role as parents in instilling in our children these beliefs, values, and ethics?

---

[4]In Lawrence A. Hoffman, ed., *My People's Prayer Book Volume 2: The Amidah* (Woodstock Vt.: Jewish Lights Publishing, 1998), p. 101.

Teaching Our Children (20 minutes)

Ask the participants to each choose one of the thirteen blessings and describe how they might want to teach the importance of this blessing to their children.

Conclusion (5–10 minutes)

1. Write the following on the board and ask each participant to share a closing thought:

   Today I learned ____________________ .

2. As a follow-up to the session, you may want to consider creating an ongoing column in the temple bulletin, which would feature one of the intermediate petitionary blessings of the *Amidah* along with commentary from the participants about the meaning of the blessing and how to teach that blessing to children.

Petitionary Blessings of the *Amidah*

Blessing 1

אַתָּה חוֹנֵן לְאָדָם דַּעַת וּמְלַמֵּד לֶאֱנוֹשׁ בִּינָה. חָנֵּנוּ מֵאִתְּךָ דֵּעָה,
בִּינָה וְהַשְׂכֵּל. בָּרוּךְ אַתָּה יי, חוֹנֵן הַדָּעַת.

By Your grace we have the power to gain knowledge and to learn wisdom. Favor us with knowledge, wisdom, and insight, for You are their Source. We praise You, O God, gracious Giver of Knowledge.

Blessing 2

הֲשִׁיבֵנוּ אָבִינוּ לְתוֹרָתֶךָ, וְקָרְבֵנוּ מַלְכֵּנוּ לַעֲבוֹדָתֶךָ, וְהַחֲזִירֵנוּ בִּתְשׁוּבָה
שְׁלֵמָה לְפָנֶיךָ. בָּרוּךְ אַתָּה יי, הָרוֹצֶה בִּתְשׁוּבָה.

Help us, our Creator, to return to Your teaching; draw us near, our Sovereign, to Your service; and bring us back into Your presence in perfect repentance. We praise You, O God: You delight in repentance.

Blessing 3

סְלַח-לָנוּ אָבִינוּ כִּי חָטָאנוּ, מְחַל-לָנוּ מַלְכֵּנוּ כִּי פָשָׁעְנוּ, כִּי מוֹחֵל
וְסוֹלֵחַ אַתָּה. בָּרוּךְ אַתָּה יי, חַנּוּן הַמַּרְבֶּה לִסְלוֹחַ.

Forgive us, our Creator for we have sinned; pardon us, our Sovereign, for we have transgressed; for You are One who pardons and forgives. We praise You, O God, gracious and quick to forgive.

Blessing 4

רְאֵה בְעָנְיֵנוּ וְרִיבָה רִיבֵנוּ, וּגְאָלֵנוּ מְהֵרָה לְמַעַן שְׁמֶךָ, כִּי גוֹאֵל חָזָק
אָתָּה. בָּרוּךְ אַתָּה יי, גוֹאֵל יִשְׂרָאֵל.

Look upon our affliction and help us in our need; O mighty Redeemer, redeem us speedily for Your name's sake. We praise You, O God, Redeemer of Israel.

Blessing 5

רְפָאֵנוּ יי וְנֵרָפֵא, הוֹשִׁיעֵנוּ וְנִוָּשֵׁעָה, וְהַעֲלֵה רְפוּאָה שְׁלֵמָה לְכָל־מַכּוֹתֵינוּ.
בָּרוּךְ אַתָּה יי, רוֹפֵא הַחוֹלִים.

Heal us, O God, and we shall be healed; save us, and we shall be saved; grant us a perfect healing for all our infirmities. We praise You, O God, Healer of the sick. (A personal prayer for one who is ill may be added here.)

Blessing 6

בָּרֵךְ עָלֵינוּ, יי אֱלֹהֵינוּ, אֶת־הַשָּׁנָה הַזֹּאת וְאֶת־כָּל־מִינֵי תְבוּאָתָהּ
לְטוֹבָה. וְתֵן בְּרָכָה עַל־פְּנֵי הָאֲדָמָה וְשַׂבְּעֵנוּ מִטּוּבֶךָ. בָּרוּךְ אַתָּה יי,
מְבָרֵךְ הַשָּׁנִים.

Bless this year for us, Eternal God: may its produce bring us well-being. Bestow Your blessing on the earth, that all Your children may share its abundance in peace. We praise You, O God, for You bless earth's seasons from year to year.

Blessing 7

תְּקַע בְּשׁוֹפָר גָּדוֹל לְחֵרוּתֵנוּ, וְשָׂא נֵס לִפְדּוֹת עֲשׁוּקֵינוּ, וְקוֹל דְּרוֹר
יִשָּׁמַע בְּאַרְבַּע כַּנְפוֹת הָאָרֶץ. בָּרוּךְ אַתָּה יי, פּוֹדֶה עֲשׁוּקִים.

Sound the great shofar to proclaim freedom, raise high the banner of liberation for the oppressed, and let the song of liberty be heard in the four corners of the earth. We praise You, O God, Redeemer of the oppressed.

Blessing 8

עַל שׁוֹפְטֵי אֶרֶץ שְׁפוֹךְ רוּחֶךָ, וְהַדְרִיכֵם בְּמִשְׁפְּטֵי צִדְקֶךָ, וּמְלוֹךְ עָלֵינוּ
אַתָּה לְבַדֶּךָ, בְּחֶסֶד וּבְרַחֲמִים. בָּרוּךְ אַתָּה יי, מֶלֶךְ אוֹהֵב צְדָקָה וּמִשְׁפָּט.

Bestow Your spirit upon the rulers of all lands; guide them that they may govern justly. Thus shall love and compassion be enthroned among us. We praise You, Eternal One, the Sovereign God who loves righteousness and justice.

Blessing 9

וְלָרִשְׁעָה אַל-תְּהִי תִקְוָה, וְהַתּוֹעִים אֵלֶיךָ יָשׁוּבוּ, וּמַלְכוּת זָדוֹן מְהֵרָה
תְּשַׁבֵּר. תַּקֵּן מַלְכוּתְךָ בְּתוֹכֵנוּ, בְּקָרוֹב בְּיָמֵינוּ לְעוֹלָם וָעֶד. בָּרוּךְ
אַתָּה יי, הַמַּשְׁבִּית רֶשַׁע מִן-הָאָרֶץ.

Let the reign of evil afflict us no more. May every errant heart find its way back to You. O help us to shatter the dominion of arrogance, to raise up a better world where virtue will ennoble the life of Your children. We praise You, O God, whose will it is that evil may vanish from the earth.

Blessing 10

עַל-הַצַּדִּיקִים וְעַל-הַחֲסִידִים וְעַל גֵּרֵי הַצֶּדֶק וְעָלֵינוּ יֶהֱמוּ רַחֲמֶיךָ,
יי אֱלֹהֵינוּ, וְתֵן שָׂכָר טוֹב לְכֹל הַבּוֹטְחִים בְּשִׁמְךָ בֶּאֱמֶת, וְשִׂים חֶלְקֵנוּ
עִמָּהֶם לְעוֹלָם. בָּרוּךְ אַתָּה יי, מִשְׁעָן וּמִבְטָח לַצַּדִּיקִים.

For the righteous and faithful of all humankind, for all who join their lives to ours, for all who put their trust in You, and for all honest men and women, we ask Your favor, Eternal God. Grant that we may always be numbered among them. We praise You, O God, Staff and Support of the righteous.

Blessing 11

שְׁכוֹן, יי אֱלֹהֵינוּ, בְּתוֹךְ יְרוּשָׁלַיִם עִירֶךָ, וִיהִי שָׁלוֹם בִּשְׁעָרֶיהָ, וְשַׁלְוָה
בְּלֵב יוֹשְׁבֶיהָ, וְתוֹרָתְךָ מִצִּיּוֹן תֵּצֵא, וּדְבָרְךָ מִירוּשָׁלָיִם. בָּרוּךְ אַתָּה יי,
בּוֹנֵה יְרוּשָׁלָיִם.

Let Your presence be manifest in Jerusalem, Your city. Establish peace in her gates and quietness in the hearts of all who dwell there. Let Your Torah go forth from Zion, Your word from Jerusalem. We praise You, O God, Builder of Jerusalem.

Blessing 12

אֶת-צֶֽמַח צְדָקָה מְהֵרָה תַצְמִֽיחַ, וְקֶֽרֶן יְשׁוּעָה תָּרוּם כִּנְאֻמֶֽךָ,
כִּי לִישׁוּעָתְךָ קִוִּֽינוּ כָּל-הַיּוֹם. בָּרוּךְ אַתָּה יי, מַצְמִֽיחַ קֶֽרֶן יְשׁוּעָה.

Let the plant of righteousness blossom and flourish, and let the light of deliverance shine forth according to Your word: we await your deliverance all the day. We praise You, O God: You will cause the light of deliverance to dawn for all the world.

Blessing 13

שְׁמַע קוֹלֵֽנוּ, יי אֱלֹהֵֽינוּ, חוּס וְרַחֵם עָלֵֽינוּ, וּתְקַבֵּל בְּרַחֲמִים וּבְרָצוֹן
אֶת-תְּפִלָּתֵֽנוּ, כִּי אֵל שׁוֹמֵֽעַ תְּפִלּוֹת וְתַחֲנוּנִים אָֽתָּה. בָּרוּךְ אַתָּה יי,
שׁוֹמֵֽעַ תְּפִלָּה.

Hear our voice, Eternal God; have compassion upon us, and accept our prayer with favor and mercy, for You are a God who hears prayer and supplication. We praise You, O God: You hearken to prayer.

Exploring the Intermediate Blessings

1. What belief, value, or ethic is reflected in each of these blessings?

2. How do you think saying the blessings might inspire positive action on your part? How might you translate the hopes expressed in blessings into realities?

3. As a group of six, rcad through these thirteen blessings again and find words that are the opposites of each other (e.g., affliction and healing, transgression and repentance, evil and righteousness). Using these word pairs, state a problem with the negative word and then create a solution with its opposite. For example:

   When I see **evil** like _______ I can work for **righteousness** by _____________.

   When I **transgress** by _______ I can **repent** by ____________________.

   When I see **affliction** like ____________ I can **heal** by __________________ .

4. What kind of Jewish life do you think is envisioned in these blessings? Prepare a statement to share with the other groups.

Text Study

Rabbi Daniel Landes has written, "Each of the middle petitionary blessings has ethical consequences for us who pray it. Since we ask God to do these things, it must be in God's nature to do them; since we are made in God's image, it must be our nature also to do them, when we act in a godly way. The middle blessings are, therefore, more than requests we make of God. They are equally a catalogue of our own responsibilities."

(IN LAWRENCE A. HOFFMAN, ED., *MY PEOPLE'S PRAYERBOOK VOLUME 2: THE AMIDAH* [WOODSTOCK, VT.: JEWISH LIGHTS PUBLISHING, 1998], P. 101)

G'milut Chasadim Session 1
Sacred Obligations: Discovering Meaning in the Mitzvot

Introduction

The focus of this session is on the mitzvot and the role they play in Jewish life, especially from the perspective of Reform Judaism. This session asks the participants to consider the meaning of the term "mitzvah" and to reflect on the mitzvah choices they have already made, including the influence of their observance on themselves and their children. Participants will also be asked to consider new mitzvot to observe.

This session includes a great deal of material and could be scheduled for a two-hour session. Consider adding extra time to the allotted times for each activity in the Session Overview.

Enduring Understanding

Nurturing a strong Jewish identity requires the active participation of parents in their children's Jewish living and learning experiences.

Essential Questions

1. Who am I as a Jewish parent and a Jewish role model?
2. How does one establish a sacred relationship between parent and child?
3. What makes a meaningful Jewish life?
4. What does it mean to be a Jewish family?

Questions to Be Addressed

1. How can observing mitzvot make Judaism more meaningful to the individual?
2. How do choices about the observance of mitzvot influence and affect families?
3. How can observing mitzvot deepen one's attachment to Judaism and make its observance more meaningful?
4. What role does the observance of mitzvot play in Reform Jewish life?

Evidence of Understanding

- Participants will identify their own mitzvah choices and the personal and potential meaning they (can) derive from observing them and introducing new ones.
- Participants will share and discuss the influence of mitzvah observances on themselves and on their families.

Session Overview

- Set Induction (15 minutes)
- Mitzvah Survey and Discussion (30–35 minutes)
- Text Study (20 minutes)
- Conclusion (10 minutes)

Materials Needed

- Photocopies of text materials and handouts (pages 136–143)
- Pens or pencils
- Chalkboard and chalk or flip chart and markers
- Pens or pencils

SESSION PLAN

Set Induction (15 minutes)

This Set Induction is designed to encourage participants to articulate their own understanding of the word "mitzvah" and to examine and reflect upon three different definitions of the term.

1. Ask participants to share with the group their understanding of the meaning of the word "mitzvah." Write their key words or phrases on the board or flip chart.
2. When the group is done, distribute the handouts on pages 136–143 and ask the participants to look at Mitzvah: Three Definitions on page 136. Invite a volunteer to read each one aloud. Ask participants to express their reactions to the definitions and ask if they can identify any one they prefer over the others. They should explain the reasons for their selections.

Mitzvah Survey and Discussion (30–35 minutes)

In this activity, participants will identify mitzvot they (and perhaps their families) are currently observing, mitzvot they would consider "trying," and mitzvot they would not want to observe. The activity involves rotation and discussion, but if this approach does not seem feasible for your session, an alternative would be to simply arrange participants in pairs or small groups for the survey review discussion.

1. Ask participants to turn to the survey The Mitzvot of Our Family on page 137. Read the survey directions aloud and ask participants to complete it.

2. After the participants have completed the survey, divide them into two groups, "Group 1" and "Group 2." Arrange chairs to form two parallel lines, so that each Group 1 member faces a Group 2 member. This arrangement will allow you to organize the group of participants into study pairs (in Hebrew, *chevruta*; pl. *chevrutot*). If there are an uneven number of participants, the group leader may join in or create one group of three.

   - Participants will discuss their responses to the survey in rotating *chevrutot*. They will choose an "A" answer and describe to their *chevruta* partners why they observe that mitzvah, articulate its importance to them personally, and explain how they came to observe that particular mitzvah.

   - After this first discussion, ask the members of Group 1 to stand; have the person at the head of the line move down to the last chair and all other Group 1 members move up one chair. New *chevrutot* are now formed. Ask participants to choose a new "A" answer from the survey and follow the previous discussion format.

   - Proceed with a third *chevruta*, having participants move along in the same manner as before, only this time they will have to choose a "B" answer. Participants will reflect on their own mitzvah choices and the personal and potential meaning they can derive from these observances.

   - Finish with a fourth *chevruta*, having participants move along in the same manner as before, only this time they will have to choose and discuss a "C" answer, reflecting on their own mitzvah choices and the decisions each individual Jew makes for himself or herself.

3. Conclude the activity by bringing the group back together as a whole and asking participants to briefly share any reactions they had to the process.

Text Study (20 minutes)

1. Divide participants into small groups of four to five people, making sure each group has a volunteer leader. Ask participants to turn to the Text Study sheet on page 139 and to review both texts and discuss their answers to the questions that follow them.

2. Reconvene as a whole group and ask the volunteer leaders from the smaller discussion groups to report on the conversations.

Conclusion (10 minutes)

Point out to the participants that making decisions about mitzvah observance requires thought, knowledge, and commitment. Our decisions about the observance of mitzvot may change over time. As our families grow and change, we may have different needs and different understandings that will affect the mitzvah choices we make. A Mitzvah Starter Kit and The Mitzvot Bibliography (pages 140–143) are resources that will help them investigate the mitzvot, their meanings, and their observances. Ask if there are any questions about these materials.

Mitzvah מִצְוָה

Three Definitions

A commandment, precept, or religious duty. The term is derived from the Hebrew root צ-ו-ה, which means "to command" or "to ordain." In common usage, mitzvah has taken on the meaning of a good deed. Already in the Talmud, this word was used for a meritorious act as distinct from a positive commandment.

(*ENCYCLOPEDIA JUDAICA*)

A mitzvah or "commandment" is a deed in which humans are given an opportunity to fulfill the will of God. That will is inherent within creation itself, as God has created a world that is not yet perfect. The claim of the mitzvah is that there is work left for us to do, work that will make us "partners of God in the world's creation," as the Midrash says it.

(RABBI ARTHUR GREEN, *THESE ARE THE WORDS: A VOCABULARY OF JEWISH SPIRITUAL LIFE* [WOODSTOCK, VT.: JEWISH LIGHTS PUBLISHING, 2000], P. 98)

Mitzvah is the key to authentic Jewish existence and to the sanctification of life. No English equivalent can adequately translate the term. Its root meaning is "commandment," but mitzvah has come to have broader meanings. It suggests the joy of doing something for the sake of others and for the sake of God, and it conveys still more: it also speaks of living Jewishly, or meeting life's challenges and opportunities in particular ways.

(SIMEON J. MASLIN, ED., *GATES OF MITZVAH: A GUIDE TO THE JEWISH LIFE CYCLE* [NEW YORK: CENTRAL CONFERENCE OF AMERICAN RABBIS, 1979], P. 3)

The Mitzvot of Our Family

Write *A* next to those mitzvot that are part of your family's current observance.
Write *B* next to those mitzvot you would consider observing.
Write *C* next to those mitzvot that you and your family would not observe.

1. _____ Preserving the environment.

2. _____ Visiting the sick.

3. _____ Being respectful to others—having good manners.

4. _____ Telling the truth.

5. _____ Welcoming the stranger.

6. _____ Returning lost property.

7. _____ Honoring father and mother.

8. _____ Celebrating *Rosh Chodesh*—the new moon.

9. _____ Visiting a sukkah (e.g., eating a meal in a sukkah).

10. _____ Putting a mezuzah on the doorpost of our home.

11. _____ Hearing the shofar on the High Holy Days.

12. _____ Not stealing.

13. _____ Not gossiping.

14. _____ Comforting mourners.

15. _____ Lighting Shabbat candles and saying the blessings.

16. _____ Saying the blessings over wine and challah for Shabbat.

17. _____ Eating matzah during Passover.

18. _____ Studying Torah and other Jewish texts.

19. _____ Praying with the community.

20. _____ Being kind to animals.

21. _____ Giving *tzedakah* (money and material goods).

22. _____ Feeding the hungry.

23. _____ Fasting on Yom Kippur.

24. _____ Participating in a Passover seder.

25. _____ Lighting Chanukah candles.

26. _____ Reciting *HaMotzi* (the blessing over bread) before eating.

27. _____ Hearing the Megillah on Purim.

28. _____ Keeping your word.

29. _____ Keeping some form of dietary laws, such as not eating pork or shellfish, not mixing meat and milk, or purchasing only kosher food products.

30. _____ Building a sukkah.

Text Study

Text 1

As Reform Jews we are "to follow those religious practices and customs that personally and authentically touch [one's] heart."

(FROM "UNPACKING THE PRINCIPLES: RESOURCES FOR BEGINNING A DISCUSSION OF 'A STATEMENT OF PRINCIPLES FOR REFORM JUDAISM,'" AVAILABLE ONLINE AT WWW.URJ.ORG/EDUCATE/PRINCIPLES/TORAH6.SHTML)

Discussion Questions

1. Which mitzvot touch your heart? What is meaningful and important to you? Which mitzvot are important for your family to observe?
2. In what ways have these observances added meaning to your life as a Jew?
3. How might mitzvah observances add meaning to the lives of your children?

Text 2

Adonai *spoke to Moses, saying: "Speak to the whole Israelite community and say to them: 'You shall be holy, for I,* Adonai *your God, am holy.'"*

(LEVITICUS 19:1–2)

Discussion Questions

1. What does it mean to bring holiness into your life?
2. Mitzvot are understood as sacred obligations. How does the observance of mitzvot bring the sacred and the holy into our lives?
3. As a parent, how do your mitzvah choices affect your children?
4. How do your children influence your mitzvah choices?
5. What influence do you want the mitzvot to have on your children?
6. Which mitzvot connect you to Judaism? Are there additional mitzvot that would strengthen those connections? Share and explain.

A Mitzvah Starter Kit

Shamor V'zachor Shabbat—Observing and Remembering Shabbat

In the Ten Commandments we are told, "Remember the Sabbath day to keep it holy. Six days you shall labor and do all your work, but the seventh day is a Sabbath of Adonai *your God: you shall not do any work. . . . For in six days the Eternal One made heaven and earth and sea, and all that is in them, and God rested on the seventh day; therefore, the Eternal One blessed the seventh day and hallowed it."*
(EXODUS 20:8–11)

Fulfilling This Mitzvah

There are many observances and celebrations that are a part of Shabbat. Here are just a few to choose from:

> Friday night dinner—kindling the lights, reciting the blessings over the wine and challah, having a Shabbat meal as a family, attending Friday evening services.
>
> Saturday—attending Shabbat morning services, participating in a Torah study session.
>
> Saturday evening—celebrating *Havdalah*, the ceremony that ends Shabbat.

Other "special" things to do in order to observe the holy day of Shabbat include inviting guests to share part of your Shabbat celebration, turning off the television and the computer and spending quality time together as a family, treating your family to something really extraordinary (e.g., cooking the family's favorite dishes, participating all together in some fun activity).

Talmud Torah—Studying Torah and Jewish Texts

In the Sh'ma *we are commanded to "Teach them [God's words, the mitzvot] faithfully to your children; speak of them in your home and on your way, when you lie down and when you rise up."*

(DEUTERONOMY 6:7) THIS IMPORTANT SENTENCE IN THE SH'MA REMINDS US OF THE PARENTS' ROLE IN THEIR CHILDREN'S JEWISH EDUCATION.

Fulfilling This Mitzvah

Children's Jewish learning begins in the home. Parents can help to model this learning in several effective ways: reading Jewish books, thus becoming themselves knowledgeable about Judaism; reading age-appropriate Jewish books to their children; bringing the children to Jewish museums or historical sites; often and freely discussing Jewish topics at the dinner table, letting children participate, and clarifying any questions they may have; or watching movies with Jewish content and afterwards commenting on them.

Tzedakah—Doing Righteous Acts

In the Torah we read: "Do that which is right and good in the sight of God" (Deuteronomy 6:18).

Rabbi Mark Washofsky explains that this commandment "requires us to act as a holy people in every aspect of our daily lives, in our contact with all our fellow human beings, in our social and economic pursuits no less than in our ritual activities."

(MARK WASHOFSKY, *JEWISH LIVING: A GUIDE TO CONTEMPORARY REFORM PRACTICE* [NEW YORK: UAHC PRESS, 2001], P. 297)

Fulfilling This Mitzvah

Feed the hungry by volunteering in a community soup kitchen or regularly buying food to donate to a local food pantry; donate clothing and other goods your family no longer needs; have a family *tzedakah* box in which small change is regularly collected—a good time to give this money to a needy person or to a good cause is just before Shabbat begins. These and all other actions that aim at fulfilling the mitzvah should be shared by the entire family; family members should be aware of them and, as much as possible, take part in carrying them out.

The Mishnah teaches, "Say little and do much" (*Pirkei Avot* 1:15). Discuss what kind of deeds a righteous person would do. Then, as a family, create a list of these deeds and post them in a prominent place in your home. Encourage family members to choose a righteous act to be performed each week. Discuss the deeds that family members do, why a particular deed was chosen, what good resulted from it, and how it affected or changed both the doer and recipient.

Bal Tashchit—Don't Destroy the Earth

In the Torah we read, "When in war against a city you have to besiege a long time in order to capture it, you must not destroy its trees, wielding the ax against them. You may eat of them, but you must not cut them down. Are trees of the field human to withdraw before you into the besieged city?"

(DEUTERONOMY 20:19)

The verse teaches us that we are not to needlessly destroy anything. This includes the environment, the earth, our possessions, and the possessions of others. We are to be caretakers of the earth and all it possesses.

The scriptural basis for this is found in the Book of Psalms: "The earth is Adonai*'s and all that it holds, the world and its inhabitants."*

(PSALMS 24:1)

Fulfilling This Mitzvah

One important way of caring for the earth is to make recycling a family priority. Check to see if your local energy company will do a home energy audit, and if possible schedule one in order to find out how you can save energy in your home. Discuss how your family can conserve or reuse things; try to find ways to avoid being wasteful or destructive, not only with regard to the environment but also of family and personal possessions. Post a list of ideas in a prominent place as a reminder.

Bikur Cholim—Visiting the Sick

According to Jewish tradition, one who visits a sick person helps him or her recover (Talmud, Nedarim *40a). The biblical basis for the mitzvah of* bikur cholim *(visiting the sick) comes from the Book of Genesis: "And Adonai appeared to him [Abraham] by the terebinths of Mamre" (Genesis 18:1). The Talmud (*Sotah *14a) explains that God visited the sick. In the case of Abraham, God visited Abraham when he was recovering from his circumcision.*

Fulfilling This Mitzvah

Make it a family habit to visit and/or send cards, prepare meals, and/or run errands for friends and family members who are ill. If there is a caring committee at your synagogue, consider becoming a member and actively participate.

The Mitzvot Bibliography

Artson, Bradley Shavit. *It's a Mitzvah: Step-by-Step to Jewish Living.* Springfield, N.J.: Behrman House; New York: The Rabbinical Assembly, 1995.

Kadden, Barbara Binder, and Bruce Kadden. *Teaching Mitzvot.* Denver: A.R.E., 1996.

Meyer, Michael A., and W. Gunter Plaut. *The Reform Judaism Reader: North American Documents.* New York: UAHC Press, 2001.

Olitzky, Kerry M., and Ronald H. Isaacs. *The How-to-Handbook for Jewish Living.* Hoboken, N.J.: KTAV Publishing House, 1993.

________. *The Second How-to-Handbook for Jewish Living.* Hoboken N.J.: KTAV Publishing House, 1996.

Shapiro, Mark Dov. *Gates of Shabbat/Shaarei Shabbat: A New Shabbat Manual for the 1990's.* New York: CCAR Press, 1990.

Washofsky, Mark. *Jewish Living: A Guide to Contemporary Reform Practice.* New York: UAHC Press, 2001.

Online resources:
clickonjudaism.org/

G'milut Chasadim Session 2
Havdalah: Reaching for the Sacred

Introduction

Shabbat concludes with *Havdalah,* a ceremony that marks the distinction between Shabbat—sacred time—and the weekday—ordinary time. "Just as Shabbat is ushered in with a ritual act of candlelighting," note Rabbis Kerry Olitzky and Daniel Judson, "so too we leave Shabbat with a similar ritual act that involves light. It is a bittersweet time. It is also a time steeped in mystery as the daylight slips into darkness."[1] The concept of separation is basic to Jewish thought, both traditional and modern: making distinctions between what is holy and what is not is central to the experience of living a Jewish life. The ceremony itself includes a blessing over sweet smelling spices, which remind us of the sweetness of Shabbat. Just as the sweet smelling spices carry us into the new week, so too does this session encourage the participants to bring sacred time into the everyday of their lives.

This session has been designed as an actual *Havdalah* experience, and for that reason, it would ideally be scheduled at the conclusion of Shabbat. It includes a *m'laveih malkah,* the light meal that is traditionally eaten after *Havdalah.* Arrangements should be made to provide the meal, either through the synagogue or by asking participants to bring a dish to share. If it is not possible to conduct the session in this way, it can be scheduled at another time as a simulation or "practice" ceremony.

This session presumes some level of knowledge about Shabbat on the part of participants. If this is not the case, you may want to give an overview of the meaning of Shabbat observance as a brief introduction. For helpful information on this subject, you can consult *Avodah* Session 1, "Shabbat: Day of Rest, Day of Wonder, Day of Peace," on page 67, or the two-session "Shabbat: A Gift of Family Time" workshop in *CHAI Early Childhood Parent Education.*

Enduring Understanding

Nurturing a strong Jewish identity requires the active participation of parents in their children's Jewish living and learning experiences.

[1]Kerry M. Olitzky and Daniel Judson, *The Rituals and Practices of a Jewish Life* (Woodstock, Vt.: Jewish Lights Publishing, 2002), p. 77.

Essential Questions

1. Who am I as a Jewish parent and a Jewish role model?
2. How does one establish a sacred relationship between parent and child?
3. What makes a meaningful Jewish life?
4. What does it mean to be a Jewish family?

Questions to Be Addressed

1. How does *Havdalah* create sacred time for the family?
2. How does one find the sacred in everyday life?
3. How can one nurture sacred time with family?

Evidence of Understanding

- Participants will share their own definitions of "sacred."
- Participants will discuss how to find and nurture sacred time.

Session Overview

- Set Induction (15 minutes)
- *Havdalah* Service (15 minutes)
- Conclusion: *M'laveih Malkah* and Discussion (45–60 minutes)

Materials Needed

- Copies of "First a Spark" and the *Havdalah* service (pages 148–153)
- *Havdalah* candle
- *Kiddush* cup (wine cup)
- Wine
- *B'samim*—sweet smelling spices, like cinnamon, cloves, and allspice, in a container that opens
- Matches

SESSION PLAN

Set Induction (15 minutes)

1. Distribute copies of "First a Spark" and the *Havdalah* service (pages 148–153) to the participants and ask a volunteer to read the poem aloud.

2. Invite discussion about the following questions:

   - A line from the poem reads, "for candles grow smaller, the children grow taller, even as we pray." What message do you think the poet is sharing?

   - What would you identify as sacred in this poem?

   - What is sacred time and space for you?

   - What have been sacred times and places for your family?

Havdalah Service (15 minutes)

The *Havdalah* service on pages 150–153 is an interweaving of explanation about *Havdalah* and a *Havdalah* service. Invite the participants to stand and gather in a circle. Although you may choose to read the ser-vice and the readings yourself, it would be preferable to go around the circle and have others take turns reading, especially the English verses. The Hebrew sections should be reserved for those who are comfortable reading Hebrew.

Conclusion: *M'laveih Malkah* and Discussion (45–60 minutes)

Share a light meal with the participants to bid the Shabbat Queen goodbye. At some point during the meal, pose the following questions for discussion:

- When we smell the *b'samim,* spices, we take some of the sweetness of Shabbat with us into the new week. What feelings and attitudes would you like to carry into the new week?

- Think over the past week. What were sacred moments for you?

- Did you share sacred moments with your family this week?

- What are the greatest challenges to finding sacred time/sacred moments for your family?

- Was there a time this week when sharing a sacred moment would have helped you in some way? If you are comfortable doing so, describe that time.

- How might *Havdalah* bring a sense of the sacred into your family life?

- What do you need so that you can observe *Havdalah* in your home?

First a Spark

by Rabbi Sandy Eisenberg Sasso*

First a spark
then candle glow.

I watched you at sunset time
eyes sparkling in Shabbat light.

Circling above the flames,
my hands pulled
the warmth of Shabbat peace inside.

Praying for a good week and for blessing.

Take time—the lights beckon
for dreams and wonder,
for candles grow smaller,
the children grow taller,
even as we pray.

Hold this sunset moment and let it go
into morning light.

Another generation's candlesticks
receive the next generation's lights.

And somewhere in the middle
we stand, holding hands
with yesterday and tomorrow,
linking echoes of ancient melodies
with the breath of our children.

Finding God and hope in their embrace,
renewing days of creation.

In ordinary time—remember—
First a spark
and then candle glow.

---

*Reprinted by permission of Rabbi Sandy Eisenberg Sasso.

Discussion Questions

1. A line from the poem reads, "for candles grow smaller, the children grow taller, even as we pray." What message do you think the poet is sharing?
2. What you would identify as sacred in this poem?
3. What is sacred time and space for you?
4. What have been sacred times and places for your family?

Havdalah Service

Havdalah moves us from the sacred time of Shabbat to the ordinary time of the weekday. Abraham Joshua Heschel describes Shabbat as a palace in time. *Havdalah* is one of the building blocks of that palace. *Havdalah* is for letting go of Shabbat; it is a sweet farewell encouraging us to take the pleasures and joys of Shabbat into the new week.

Havdalah begins with seven verses that come from the biblical books of Isaiah, Esther, and Psalms. These verses remind us of our relationship with God; they express our thanks for the blessings that fill our lives and our hopes for the coming week.

Behold, God is my Help;
trusting in the Eternal One, I am not afraid.
For the Eternal One is my strength and my song,
and has become my salvation.
With joy we draw water
from the wells of salvation.
The Eternal One brings deliverance,
and blessing to the people.
The God of the hosts of heaven is with us;
the God of Jacob is our stronghold.
God of the hosts of heaven,
happy is the one who trusts in You!
Save us, Eternal One;
answer us, when we call upon You.
Give us light and joy, gladness and honor,
as in the happiest days of our people's past.
Then shall we lift up the cup to rejoice in Your saving power,
and call out Your name in praise.

We begin and end Shabbat by blessing wine, a symbol of joy and gladness. We fill the *Havdalah* wine cup to the brim, a symbol of the bounty we hope to enjoy in the coming week.

Raise the cup of wine or juice and say:

בָּרוּךְ אַתָּה יי אֱלֹהֵינוּ מֶלֶךְ הָעוֹלָם, בּוֹרֵא פְּרִי הַגָּפֶן.

Baruch atah Adonai, Eloheinu melech haolam, borei p'ri hagafen.

We praise You, Eternal God, Sovereign of the universe, Creator of the fruit of the vine.

B'samim are spices, which represent the sweetness of Shabbat. The Rabbis teach us that each Jew receives an additional soul—a *n'shamah y'teirah*, a kind of added spirituality—in honor of Shabbat. When Shabbat ends, this *n'shamah* leaves us, and we try to find consolation for her loss in the scent of these sweet spices.

Raise the spice box and say:

בָּרוּךְ אַתָּה יי אֱלֹהֵינוּ מֶלֶךְ הָעוֹלָם, בּוֹרֵא מִינֵי בְשָׂמִים.

Baruch atah Adonai, Eloheinu melech haolam, borei minei v'samim.

We praise You, Eternal God, Sovereign of the universe, Creator of types of spices.

(Circulate the spice box and let each participant inhale its fragrance.)

God's first creation was light. As we begin our new week we also create light with the *Havdalah* candle. We bless this light by praising God as the creator of the lights of fire. These lights of fire are represented by the *Havdalah* candle, which has many wicks. We turn the back of our hands toward the lit *Havdalah* candle and bend our fingers as if making an open fist, letting the light reflect on our fingernails. In so doing we observe the commandment to make use of the *Havdalah* light. And the shadows created by our fingers on our palms remind us of the distinction between light and darkness, for *Havdalah* is about making distinctions—distinctions between light and darkness, Shabbat and the weekday, the holy and the everyday.

Hold up the lit *Havdalah* candle and say:

בָּרוּךְ אַתָּה יי אֱלֹהֵינוּ מֶלֶךְ הָעוֹלָם, בּוֹרֵא מְאוֹרֵי הָאֵשׁ.

Baruch atah Adonai, Eloheinu melech haolam, borei m'orei haeish.

We praise You, Eternal God, Sovereign of the universe, Creator of the lights of fire.

Hold the *Havdalah* candle high and say:

בָּרוּךְ אַתָּה יי אֱלֹהֵינוּ מֶלֶךְ הָעוֹלָם, הַמַּבְדִּיל בֵּין
קֹדֶשׁ לְחוֹל, בֵּין אוֹר לְחֹשֶׁךְ, בֵּין יִשְׂרָאֵל
לָעַמִּים, בֵּין יוֹם הַשְּׁבִיעִי לְשֵׁשֶׁת יְמֵי הַמַּעֲשֶׂה.

Baruch atah Adonai, Eloheinu melech haolam, hamavdil bein kodesh l'chol, bein or l'choshech, bein yisrael la-amim, bein yom hash'vi-i l'sheishet y'mei hamaaseh.

We praise You, Eternal God, Sovereign of the universe: You make distinctions, teaching us to distinguish the commonplace from the holy; You create light and darkness, Israel and the nations, the seventh day of rest, and the six days of labor.

We praise God for separating and distinguishing the holy from the common, Shabbat from the six days of labor.

בָּרוּךְ אַתָּה יי אֱלֹהֵנוּ מֶלֶךְ הָעוֹלָם, הַמַּבְדִּיל בֵּין קֹדֶשׁ לְחוֹל.

Baruch atah Adonai, Eloheinu melech haolam, hamavdil bein kodesh l'chol.

We praise You, O God: You call us to distinguish the commonplace from the holy.

(All participants drink from the wine cup.)

We extinguish the *Havdalah* candle in the wine or juice by immersing it in the *Kiddush* cup.

May we take the peace and beauty of Shabbat with us into the new week, wishing each other a *Shavua Tov*—a good week:

Sing:

שָׁבוּעַ טוֹב ...

Shavuah tov, Shavuah tov, Shavuah tov, Shavuah tov.

A good week, a week of peace; may gladness reign and joy increase.

Shabbat is a foretaste of a very special time—the messianic era—the world to come, a world filled with peace, blessing, and understanding. In Jewish tradition, it is Elijah the Prophet who will herald that time.

אֵלִיָּהוּ הַנָּבִיא, אֵלִיָּהוּ הַתִּשְׁבִּי, אֵלִיָּהוּ, אֵלִיָּהוּ, אֵלִיָּהוּ הַגִּלְעָדִי
בִּמְהֵרָה בְיָמֵינוּ, יָבֹא אֵלֵינוּ, עִם מָשִׁיחַ בֶּן דָּוִד, עִם מָשִׁיחַ
בֶּן דָּוִד. אֵלִיָּהוּ הַנָּבִיא...

Eiliyahu hanavi, Eiliyahu hatishbi,
Eiliyahu, Eiliyahu, Eiliyahu hagiladi.
Bim'heira v'yameinu, yavo eileinu, im Mashiach ben David, im Mashiach ben David.
Eiliyahu hanavi, Eiliyahu hatishbi,
Eiliyahu, Eiliyahu, Eiliyahu hagiladi.

Elijah the prophet, the Tishbite, the Gileadite: come to us soon, to herald our redemption.

There is an old custom of saying farewell to Shabbat by having a special meal after the *Havdalah* ceremony. It is called *m'laveih malkah* and means "escorting out the Shabbat Queen." The image of Shabbat as a queen or bride is found in the Talmud. It is written that on the eve of Shabbat, at twilight, Rabbi Chanina used to wrap himself in a special robe, stand up, and say, "Come, let us go forth to welcome Queen Sabbath" (Babylonian Talmud, *Shabbat* 119a). Another greeting used to welcome the Shabbat was "Come, bride; come, bride."

The mystics of sixteenth-century Safed developed the tradition of going out to the fields to welcome the Sabbath using the imagery of welcoming a bride or queen in their songs and poems. This observance of the kabbalists laid the foundation for *Kabbalat Shabbat*—the welcoming of Shabbat. On *Erev Shabbat,* the eve of the Sabbath, we welcome the Sabbath Queen, and on Saturday evening we say goodbye to the Sabbath Queen, escorting her out through a farewell meal. The *m'laveih malkah* meal is also known as "King David's meal." In the Bible, we read that King David wanted to know from God the day of his death: "Tell me, *Adonai,* what my term is, what is the measure of my days." According to a Talmudic legend, God replied that he would die on a Shabbat. So, at the end of each Shabbat, King David held a feast to celebrate the fact that he was going to live another week. May we all live this week in peace, joy, and love.

Bibliography (for further reading about Shabbat and *Havdalah)*

Elkins, Dov Peretz. *A Shabbat Reader: Universe of Cosmic Joy.* New York: UAHC Press, 1998.

Heschel, Abraham Joshua. *The Sabbath: Its Meaning for Modern Man.* New York: Farrar, Straus and Giroux, 1980.

Perelson, Ruth. *An Invitation to Shabbat: A Beginner's Guide to Weekly Celebration.* New York: UAHC Press, 1997.

Shapiro, Mark Dov. *Gates of Shabbat/Shaarei Shabbat: A New Shabbat Manual for the 1990's.* New York: CCAR Press, 1990.

Stern, Chaim, ed. *On The Doorposts of Your House: Prayers and Ceremonies for the Jewish Home.* New York: Central Conference of American Rabbis, 1994.

G'milut Chasadim Session 3 *Sh'lom Bayit:* Creating a Shelter of Peace

INTRODUCTION

"One of the primary reasons for adding a consistent Jewish dimension to family life," observes noted author Anita Diamant, "is to create opportunities for sharing moments of peace."[1] *Sh'lom bayit* means "peace of the home." Traditionally, the Jewish home was considered a *mikdash m'at,* a little sanctuary, a place of peace and tranquility in an often chaotic and inhospitable outside environment. In our fast-paced, over-programmed world, home should still be a place to turn to for comfort, love, and respite from the stresses and pressures of everyday life. This is an essential Jewish value. The purpose of this session is to learn about this Jewish value and to foster in the participants the ability to create a home defined by *sh'lom bayit.*

There are a variety of activities and discussions included in this session along with a take-home activity. The take-home activity enables parents to teach what they have learned to their children and lays the foundation for family members to become active partners in the process of creating *sh'lom bayit.*

ENDURING UNDERSTANDING

Nurturing a strong Jewish identity requires the active participation of parents in their children's Jewish living and learning experiences.

ESSENTIAL QUESTIONS

1. Who am I as a Jewish parent and a Jewish role model?
2. How does one establish a sacred relationship between parent and child?
3. What makes a meaningful Jewish life?
4. What does it mean to be a Jewish family?

QUESTIONS TO BE ADDRESSED

1. What does *sh'lom bayit* mean?
2. What are the characteristics of *sh'lom bayit?*

[1] Anita Diamant with Howard Cooper, *Living a Jewish Life* (New York: HarperCollins, 1991), p. 23.

3. How does one create *sh'lom bayit*?
4. How can family members contribute to building *sh'lom bayit*?
5. What Jewish observances and rituals can contribute to *sh'lom bayit*?

Evidence of Understanding

- Participants will create a personal description of *sh'lom bayit.*
- Participants will share examples of *sh'lom bayit.*
- Participants will describe ways in which they can foster a climate of *sh'lom bayit* in their homes.
- Participants will give examples of Jewish observances and rituals they view as contributing to *sh'lom bayit.*

Session Overview

- Set Induction (10 minutes)
- Text Study (15 minutes)
- Our *Sh'lom Bayit* Stories (20–30 minutes)
- Building *Sh'lom Bayit* (10–15 minutes)
- Conclusion (10–15 minutes)

Materials Needed

- Photocopies of all texts and handouts (pages 159–163)
- Chalkboard and chalk or flip chart and markers

SESSION PLAN

Set Induction (10 minutes)

1. Prior to the session, write the following quote on chart paper, but do not post it until the group is ready to begin:

> The peace of the house is really the health of the house. . . . *Shalom* comes from the root *shalem*, which means "complete" or "whole." *Sh'lom bayit* is not a quiet home, but a whole one.[2]

[2]Ibid, p. 25.

2. Ask a volunteer to read the quote aloud and invite discussion about these questions, writing key words on the board or on a flip chart.

   - How would you define a peaceful, loving home?

   - What are some of the key words that describe a peaceful and loving home environment?

3. Explain to participants that this session will focus on the Jewish value of *sh'lom bayit* and how to achieve it.

Text Study (15 minutes)

1. If there are more than ten participants, divide the group into smaller groups of five to seven participants each. Distribute the handouts on pages 159–163 and ask participants to look at the text on page 159. Before beginning the discussion, explain to the participants the context of the text they will be examining: Abraham has just welcomed three strangers into his home. These strangers turn out to be divine messengers, who have come to inform Abraham that he and Sarah will become parents. Sarah, eavesdropping, finds this a little hard to believe given their advanced ages.

   > They said to him, "Where is your wife Sarah?" And he replied, "There, in the tent." Then one said, "I will return to you when life is due, and your wife Sarah shall have a son!" Sarah was listening at the entrance of the tent, which was behind him. Now Abraham and Sarah were old, advanced in years; Sarah had stopped having the periods of women. And Sarah laughed to herself, saying, "Now that I am withered, am I to have enjoyment with my husband so old?" Then *Adonai* said to Abraham, "Why did Sarah laugh, saying, 'Shall I in truth bear a child, old as I am?' " (Genesis 18: 9–13)

2. In their smaller groups, ask the participants to respond to these questions:

   - What did Sarah say when she heard the strangers' prediction? To whom was she speaking? From the text, who overhears her?

   - How did *Adonai* change her words in discussing this with Abraham?

   - Why do you think her words were changed?

3. Bring the participants back together as a whole group and explain to them that from the Talmud, we learn: "The whole Torah exists only for the sake of peace. For the sake of peace, truth may be sacrificed" (*Gittin* 59b, *Y'vamot* 65b). In light of this, discuss the following questions:

   - How did *Adonai* choose to help maintain peace between Abraham and Sarah?

   - How might this principle apply in our own families?

Our *Sh'lom Bayit* Stories (20–30 minutes)

1. Divide the whole group into smaller groups once again.

2. Turn to the *Sh'lom Bayit* Scenarios on pages 160–161 and ask participants to answer the questions. Ask them to then share their own stories and examples of *sh'lom bayit* from their family experiences, if they are comfortable doing so.

3. Bring the group back together as a whole and ask what the participants learned about *sh'lom bayit* from reviewing the scenarios.

4. Ask them to consider as a group: Based on your conversations, what helps in creating *sh'lom bayit*? What prevents it?

Building *Sh'lom Bayit* (10–15 minutes)

1. Ask participants to work in pairs to create a definition of *Sh'lom Bayit* that is meaningful for them, utilizing the following sentence completion: "A home with *sh'lom bayit* is a home in which ________________."

2. Direct the participants to write their definitions on a sheet of paper.

3. Ask one member of each working pair to read the definition the pair created.

4. Display the definitions on a bulletin board after they are read.

Conclusion (10–15 minutes)

1. Gather the participants together, directing them to sit in a circle, so that they can see each other. Ask them to verbally respond to the following open-ended statement: "To build *sh'lom bayit* for my family, I can ________________." Ask them to use a new idea or one from the previous discussion. Ask everyone to jot down all the answers that are given for use in the take-home activity.

2. Ask participants to turn to the Building Blocks of *Sh'lom Bayit* activity on page 162. Review the directions with them so they will understand how to do this activity at home with their children.

Text Study

Text 1

They said to him, "Where is your wife Sarah?" And he replied, "There, in the tent." Then one said, "I will return to you when life is due, and your wife Sarah shall have a son!" Sarah was listening at the entrance of the tent, which was behind him. Now Abraham and Sarah were old, advanced in years; Sarah had stopped having the periods of women. And Sarah laughed to herself, saying, "Now that I am withered, am I to have enjoyment with my husband so old?" Then Adonai said to Abraham, "Why did Sarah laugh, saying, 'Shall I in truth bear a child, old as I am?'"

(GENESIS 18:9–13)

Discussion Questions

1. What did Sarah say when she heard the stranger's prediction? To whom was she speaking? From the text, who overhears her?
2. How did *Adonai* change her words in discussing this with Abraham?
3. Why do you think her words were changed?

Text 2

From the Talmud, we learn: "The whole Torah exists only for the sake of peace. For the sake of peace, truth may be sacrificed."

(*GITTIN* 59B, *Y'VAMOT* 65B)

Discussion Questions

1. How did *Adonai* choose to help maintain peace between Abraham and Sarah?
2. How do we maintain peace in our families?

Sh'lom Bayit Scenarios

Scenario 1

In the 1930s, when my mother was a young girl, she sat one evening doing her homework at the big dining room table in her parents' apartment. Her mother, a seamstress, was also working that evening at the same table, cutting out a wedding gown from a cream colored silk. In those days, there weren't easy-to-use ballpoint pens that come with their own supply of ink, but fountain pens. A fountain pen had to be regularly refilled with ink. During the evening's homework session, my mother had opened a bottle of ink and filled her pen. Unfortunately she didn't close the bottle. You can probably guess what happened next. She reached over for something, bumping the bottle of ink and tipping it over. All eyes turned to the spreading puddle of blue ink on that cream colored silk. Without uttering a word my grandfather quickly picked my mother up and ran out the apartment with her. They took a long drive and returned home a couple of hours later.

- How did the grandfather's actions contribute to *sh'lom bayit* in this family?

Scenario 2

For years, the Ross family had been fighting about when to leave for synagogue on Shabbat mornings. The parents wanted to get there when the service began, but as the children got older, they wanted to sleep later on Saturday mornings and couldn't understand why they were forced to go at all. They usually managed to get ready slowly, making the family late every time.

- How could the Ross family deal with this issue to maintain *sh'lom bayit?*

Scenario 3

Mrs. Amishay wants to start celebrating Shabbat in the home by having a nice dinner every Friday night. She thinks this will be especially good for the children to reinforce what they are learning in religious school. Mr. Amishay never seems to be able to get home in time on Friday nights and this is causing tension between the parents.

- What alternatives could the family come up with to promote *sh'lom bayit* in this case?

Scenario 4

All of Amanda's friends are going on the high school trip to France this spring break. Her family has had a terrible year financially and simply can't afford to send her. Amanda is furious at her family because they all took an expensive vacation to Mexico just last year and she's ashamed to explain to her friends that the family is "too poor" to send her on the school trip.

- How can the family come to an understanding that will promote *sh'lom bayit* in this situation?

Building Blocks of *Sh'lom Bayit*

Materials Needed

- Magazines and newspapers
- Glue stick
- Scissors
- Crayons, markers, and pencils
- Drawing paper

Directions

1. Explain the concept of *sh'lom bayit* to your children, sharing what you learned in the parent education session.
2. As a family, look at the Building Blocks of *Sh'lom Bayit* handout. Ask the members of your family if they agree that the Building Blocks that are shown help build *sh'lom bayit.* Add any of your family's own ideas in the blank blocks and draw more if you need them.
3. Share with your family that they are going to illustrate their ideas about ways to create *sh'lom bayit* by making a special art project—a collage of their ideas about *sh'lom bayit.*
4. Draw a simple outline of a house on a large sheet of paper.
5. Hand out scissors, glue sticks, magazines, and newspapers. Help each other find pictures and words in the magazines and newspapers that represent the building blocks of *sh'lom bayit*, or use the Building Blocks from the handout, or a combination of both.
6. Start cutting and gluing, imagining that the words and pictures are like actual building blocks. Glue these and the building blocks onto the drawing of the house.
7. Try to find enough pictures and words to fill in the entire house drawing.
8. As the family is working on this collage, talk about how each of you envisions making the Building Blocks actions that can be carried out.

Building Blocks of *Sh'lom Bayit*

I can do a better job of cleaning up after myself.

I can listen carefully when someone is speaking to me. I can try to understand that person's feelings.

I can let my family members know that I love them.

I can be helpful without complaining.

I can admit when I make a mistake. I can forgive others for their mistakes.

I can remember to speak kindly to the people in my family.

G'milut Chasadim Session 4 Sustaining the World through Torah, Worship, and Deeds of Loving-Kindness

Introduction

In *Pirkei Avot* we learn that the world is sustained by three things: Torah, *avodah*, and *g'milut chasadim*. At their simplest these words translate as follows: Torah refers to the study of Torah itself; *avodah* means worship, and *g'milut chasadim* are acts of loving-kindness. This parent session is devoted to exploring these concepts, their meanings, and how they sustain the world. This session includes text study, discussion, and hands-on activities. Additionally, there are two take-home projects to enable and empower parents to become teachers of their own children. The first project will be started during the session and completed at home. The second project will be explained and the directions sent home with the participants. You may want to share with the parents that the *CHAI: Learning for Jewish Life Curriculum Core* is based upon the three strands of Torah, *Avodah*, and *G'milut Chasadim*.

Since many of our families are familiar with the song "Al Shlosha D'varim," it would be an enhancement to have it playing as participants assemble for the session.

Enduring Understanding

Nurturing a strong Jewish identity requires the active participation of parents in their children's Jewish living and learning experiences.

Essential Questions

1. Who am I as a Jewish parent and a Jewish role model?

2. How does one establish a sacred relationship between parent and child?

3. What makes a meaningful Jewish life?

4. What does it mean to be a Jewish family?

Questions to Be Addressed

1. Why did the Rabbis say that Torah, *avodah*, and *g'milut chasadim* are the three factors that sustain the world?

2. What is the role of the individual in sustaining the world?

3. How does one become involved in sustaining the world through Torah, *avodah,* and *g'milut chasadim?*

4. How can we involve our children and families in Torah, *avodah,* and *g'milut chasadim?*

Evidence of Understanding

- Participants will discuss the Jewish concepts of Torah, *avodah,* and *g'milut chasadim* in relation to sustaining the world.
- Participants will share their thoughts and beliefs on how the world is sustained.
- Participants will discuss the role of the individual in relation to Torah, *avodah,* and *g'milut chasadim* and sustaining the world.

Session Overview

- Set Induction (20 minutes)
- Text Study (40–45 minutes)
- Conclusion (15–20 minutes)

Materials Needed

- Inflatable globe (usually available in teacher supply stores)
- A tripod (a camera tripod, a tripod built from blocks, or a three-legged stool with removable legs)
- Chalkboard and chalk or flip chart and markers
- "Al Shlosha D'varim," available on *The Complete NFTY Recordings 1972–1989* (Transcontinental Music Publications 950103)
- Photocopies of all text and handouts (pages 168–173)
- Construction paper

SESSION PLAN

Set Induction (20 minutes)

1. If you played the song "Al Shlosha D'varim" as participants were assembling, ask they if they are familiar with the words and if they know their meaning. If you didn't play the song, begin with step 2.

2. Set the globe on the tripod. Ask the participants "If I remove one side of the tripod what will happen?" Wait for responses, then remove one side of the tripod—proving that yes, the structure will collapse and the globe will tumble to the floor.

3. Share with the participants that sustaining or supporting the world is a balancing act. Ask the participants what they feel is needed to sustain the world, letting them know that their answers can include material goods, values, ethics, or anything else that comes to mind. Record their responses on the chalkboard or flip chart. Keep the responses on the board, as they will be used in the summary discussion.

4. Share with the participants that centuries ago a Jewish teaching was written stating what sustains the world:

   > Simon the Righteous was one of the last of the Great Assembly. He used to say: The world stands on three things: on the Torah, on *avodah* (the service [of God]), on *g'milut chasadim* (acts of loving-kindness). (*Pirkei Avot* 1:2)

   Explain that *Pirkei Avot,* meaning "Chapters of the Fathers," is a book of ethical teachings that appears in the Mishnah, a compilation of Jewish teachings from the second century C.E. Simon the Righteous was a member of the Great Assembly, a group of 120 elders who became the leaders and teachers of Torah at the end of the era of the prophets, after the destruction of the First Temple.

Text Study (40–45 minutes)

In this activity, the participants will be studying three text pieces, one on each of the three pillars that sustain the world: Torah, *avodah,* and *g'milut chasadim.* There are discussion questions accompanying each text piece.

1. Divide the participants into groups of three. Distribute the handouts on pages 168–173 to the participants and direct them to read and discuss Text 1 on page 169.

2. After 12–15 minutes, ask the participants to rearrange their triads, so that no original group of three remains, and direct the new triads to read and discuss Text 2. Repeat the procedure for Text 3.

Conclusion (15–20 minutes)

1. Ask the participants to consider the answers they gave at the beginning of the session to the question, What are the things that are needed to sustain the world? (These should be on the board from the Set Induction activity.) In what ways is the teaching "the world is sustained by three things: Torah, *avodah,* and *g'milut chasadim*" timeless?

2. Ask the participants:

   - How would you suggest we build and strengthen each of these legs upon which the world stands?

   - When it comes to Torah, *avodah,* and *g'milut chasadim,* what do you want your children to know and to do? What is your role in helping them achieve these things?

3. Review the Family Project on pages 172–173. Give participants construction paper and have them create the paper model. Encourage them to complete the Family Project at home with their children.

The World Stands on Three Things

Simon the Righteous was one of the last of the Great Assembly. He used to say: The world stands on three things: on the Torah, on avodah *(the service [of God]), and on* g'milut chasadim *(acts of loving-kindness).*

(*PIRKEI AVOT* 1:2)

Text Study

Text 1: *Al HaTorah*—Upon Torah

Torah can be understood as the Five Books of the Torah or as the whole body of Jewish scholarship. In the commentary *Tosafot Yom Tov,* the word "Torah" means the duty to study Torah.

The corner-stone of the Torah . . . is to strengthen in the human heart the quality of mercy and love, to remove confidence in our own power and in the might of our hands, and to put our trust in divine Providence [God] which follows not intelligence but justice and loving kindness and sincerity.

(S. D. LUZZATTO, *YESODE HATORAH,* 1880, IN JOSEPH L. BARON, ED., *A TREASURY OF JEWISH QUOTATIONS* [NEW REV. ED.] [SOUTH BRUNSWICK, N.J.: A. S. BARNES AND CO., INC., 1965], P. 506)

Discussion Questions

1. What do you think Torah meant to Luzzatto?
2. What does Torah mean to you?
3. How can you apply your understanding of Torah to its role in sustaining the world?

Text 2: *Al HaAvodah*—Upon Worship

There are several ways to understand the Hebrew word *avodah.* These include "worship," "work," and "the sacrificial service of the Temple." Once the Temple was destroyed, prayer came to replace the sacrificial service. The Rambam (Rabbi Moses ben Maimon, a twelfth century rabbi and scholar) taught that this term meant the mitzvot (commandments).

A.
True worship is not a petition to God: it is a sermon to our own selves.

(E. G. HIRSCH, *REFORM ADVOCATE,* 1892)

B.
. . . prayer makes a difference because it sends us forth to lead lives that we might easily take for granted. It tells us that the world is good, that we should see its sanctity, and that we have a role to play in making it better. Prayer portrays an alternative world of experience that belies the humdrum view that often assails us. It lets us appreciate the miracle of life. And it lets us glimpse another reality as well: a world enhanced by the tiny acts of goodness that we are capable of, day in and day out.

(LAWRENCE A. HOFFMAN, *THE WAY INTO JEWISH PRAYER* [WOODSTOCK, VT.: JEWISH LIGHTS PUBLISHING, 2000], P. 133)

Discussion Question

If prayer is a sermon to ourselves, what messages or attitudes have you gotten from prayer or have been inspired by prayer? If this is a new idea to you, how can prayer change us in ways that will positively affect the world?

Text 3: *Al G'milut Chasadim*—Upon Acts of Loving-Kindness

G'milut means acts or deeds.
Chesed (pl. *chasidim*) may be translated as grace, kindness, or loving-kindness.

A.
In a city where there are both Jews and Gentiles, the collectors of charity collect both from Jews and from Gentiles; they feed the poor of both, visit the sick of both, bury both, comfort the mourners whether Jews or Gentiles, and they restore the lost goods of both—for the sake of peace.

(JERUSALEM TALMUD, *DEMMAI* 4:6)

B.
Because of [loving] kindness the world abides.

(RASHI—RABBI SHLOMO YITZHAKI, TENTH CENTURY FRENCH SCHOLAR AND RABBI)

Discussion Questions

1. How do the attitudes and teachings expressed by this teaching from the Talmud and by Rashi's words help us understand *g'milut chasadim* and its role in sustaining the world?

2. What do you think is the significance of the Talmud clearly stating that regardless of faith Jews are to extend *g'milut chasadim* to everyone?

3. What are the implications for us today when we engage in acts of *g'milut chasadim?*

Family Project

Learning Activity 1: Sustaining the World

1. Fold a piece of construction paper into thirds. The folded construction paper will be able to stand up, like a card. If you want, cut a design or pattern into the upper edge of the paper.

2. Write on the card the following:

On the outer fold:	The world is sustained	
On the inner fold:	by three things	
Interior:	left section:	Torah—Study
	inner section:	*Avodah*—Worship
	right side:	*G'milut chasadim*—Acts of Loving-Kindness

3. Explain that a Jewish teacher from long ago taught that the world is sustained (exists or endures) because of three things: Torah, *avodah* (worship or prayer), and *g'milut chasadim* (acts of loving-kindness).

4. Ask your children to brainstorm activities that constitute acts of Torah study, *avodah* (worship, prayer, commandments), and *g'milut chasadim* (acts of loving-kindness). You or one of your children should act as secretary and write the responses the family gives in the correct sections. Refer to the ideas generated during text study and the summary discussion.

Learning Activity 2: Turning Words into Action

1. Have your family read over the list of activities they suggested in Activity 1. Use the following questions for family discussion:

- What area would you like to work in first: Torah, *avodah,* or *g'milut chasadim?*
- What activity within that area would you like to do?

It is important that each family member share his or her thoughts and ideas on why a particular activity should be chosen. Discuss what the best activity would be for your family. The family can vote or voice consensus to decide on the first activity.

2. With members of the family, create an action plan to carry out the chosen activity.

3. Evaluate your family's experiences. This is an important step for families to connect Jewish learning with Jewish "doing." These are discussion starter questions to share with your family:

   - What did you learn by participating in this activity?
   - In what ways do you think the activity helped to sustain the world?
   - What most impressed you about this activity and what we did?
   - How did you benefit from participating in this activity?
   - What else would you like to do from the list we thought up?

G'milut Chasadim Session 5
Difference Can Be Our Strength: Becoming a Welcoming Community

INTRODUCTION

Our synagogues are populated by a wonderful diversity of individuals. Congregation members come in a variety of shapes, sizes, abilities, and orientations. Families may have two parents—a mother and a father, or two fathers or two mothers; families may have one parent, or foster parents or grandparents raising children. These families bring diversity along with challenges and benefits to a congregation. The strength of a community is reflected in its ability to reach out, welcome, and embrace this diversity. This session focuses on the role that congregants play in responding to diversity and difference. The session includes large and small discussion groups, text study, and the writing of a personal vision statement. The text study looks at two mitzvot: *hachnasat orchim*, welcoming guests/showing hospitality, and *ahavat reiacha*, loving one's neighbor. The vision statement is a personal reflection on the issues of difference and diversity and the role that the participant sees for himself or herself in fostering a warm and welcoming environment in the synagogue. The session concludes with a handout for the participants to take home and work through with their families.

For a perspective on how this subject is handled with children, you may want to refer to *G'milut Chasadim* Lesson 3, "Accepting Differences: Love Your Neighbor as Yourself," in the *CHAI Level 4 Curriculum Core.*

ENDURING UNDERSTANDING

Nurturing a strong Jewish identity requires the active participation of parents in their children's Jewish living and learning experiences.

ESSENTIAL QUESTIONS

1. Who am I as a Jewish parent and a Jewish role model?
2. How does one establish a sacred relationship between parent and child?
3. What makes a meaningful Jewish life?
4. What does it mean to be a Jewish family?

Questions to Be Addressed

1. What does Judaism have to say about welcoming guests (showing hospitality) and about loving one's neighbor?
2. How do we apply the Jewish values of welcoming guests (showing hospitality) and loving one's neighbor to the operation of our congregation?
3. How do we build and maintain bridges of understanding from member to member in our congregation?

Evidence of Understanding

- Participants will identify welcoming guests (showing hospitality) and loving one's neighbor as Jewish values.
- Participants will discuss how to reach out, welcome, and embrace the diversity and difference found in our congregations.
- Participants will create a personal vision statement on their role in creating a warm and welcoming congregation.

Session Overview

- Set Induction (30 minutes)
- Text Study (25–30 minutes)
- Vision Statement (15–20 minutes)
- Conclusion (5–10 minutes)

Materials Needed

- Photocopies of all handouts (pages 179–187)
- Poster board
- Markers
- Notepaper
- Attractive paper or stationery
- Pens or pencils

SESSION PLAN

Set Induction (30 minutes)

1. Prior to the session, reproduce the scenarios on pages 179–180 on large sheets of poster board.

2. Divide the participants into small groups of eight to ten participants each. Ask each small group to read one of the scenarios, put themselves into the shoes of the scenario character(s), and brainstorm what they believe would be the needs of that particular family as it relates to the synagogue and Jewish life.

3. Provide each group with one scenario and a marking pen. Have one person in each group record the responses of the participants on the poster board. Allow 10–15 minutes for reading and discussion. Follow up with the whole group reconvening to share what they have discussed. Allow approximately 15 minutes for these presentations.

4. Hang the scenario posters in the room.

5. When the participants have completed their responses, reconvene as one large group. Discuss the following questions:

   - Though the scenarios present different kinds of families, how are their needs similar?

   - Do any of the needs identified in the scenarios also apply to your own family?

Text Study (25–30 minutes)

1. Explain to the group that there are several mitzvot (commandments or sacred obligations) that teach us the Jewish requirements for personal interaction. We will study two Jewish texts and use the accompanying questions for discussion in order to learn about the Jewish values of welcoming guests (showing hospitality) and loving one's neighbor.

2. Distribute the handouts on pages 179–187 and ask participants to look at the texts on pages 181–183. Ask the participants to go back to their small discussion groups of eight to ten and read the texts and discuss the questions that follow. There should be one discussion leader for each group and someone who will take notes.

3. When the groups have finished their discussions, reconvene and ask:

   - What is the message behind the mitzvot?

   - What are the implications of these mitvot for us as individuals and for us as a congregation?

Vision Statement (15–20 minutes)

This summary activity will give participants an opportunity to synthesize their learning, beliefs, and attitudes about the issues of diversity and the Jewish mitzvot of *hachnasat orchim* and *ahavat reiacha*. Each participant will create a personal vision statement about his or her individual role in creating and fostering a warm and welcoming presence within the congregational community.

1. Remind participants that they have now studied the mitzvot of welcoming guests/showing hospitality *(hachnasat orchim)* and loving one's neighbor *(ahavat reiacha)* and have read and discussed scenarios that deal with difference and diversity faced by many congregations. Ask them to take a few moments to think about the application of the mitzvot they studied to the issues of difference and diversity.

2. Distribute the attractive stationery and ask each participant to synthesize his or her thoughts by writing a personal vision statement about his or her personal role in creating and fostering a warm and welcoming congregation.

Conclusion (5–10 minutes)

1. Tell the participants that there is a Yiddish expression that teaches, "What a child says on the street was first heard at home." The beliefs and attitudes that children express are born and nurtured in their homes. These beliefs and attitudes form a child's view of the world and his or her behavior. What we do and say as parents have a tremendous impact on our children. If we wish for our children to be accepting of diversity and difference, we must model that behavior for our children. If we wish for our children to be part of a warm and welcoming congregation, we as parents need to demonstrate and foster those behaviors.

2. Ask the following wrap-up questions for discussion:

   - How are we examples for our children?

   - How did you come to the values, behaviors, and attitudes by which you live your life? Who or what has had an effect on you regarding issues of difference and diversity?

   - What effect might your values, behaviors, and attitudes be having on your children?

3. Review The Mitzvot of Welcoming Guests and Loving One's Neighbor (pages 184–186) and the Family Activity Ideas (page 187) and encourage the participants to take them home and share them with their families.

Scenarios

Scenario A

Susan and her husband Mark have just moved 1,500 miles to come to our community. They have three small children, aged fifteen months, and four and seven years. A terrific job opportunity for Mark prompted the move, but they have left behind friends and family. Susan would like to go back to work part-time as an accountant. They have joined our congregation because they want a synagogue to attend on holidays, a way to find connections in their new community, and a religious school for their son.

What are the needs of this family in terms of the religious school and synagogue?

Scenario B

Anne, a Jew-by-birth, and her partner, Carole, an African American non-Jew, have recently become the parents of a biracial child. They have decided to affiliate with the congregation so that their son will be raised within the Jewish community. Carole is contemplating becoming Jewish.

What are the needs of this family in terms of the religious school and synagogue?

Scenario C

Herb, a founding member of our congregation, is facing several challenges. He is seventy-two years old and his wife has recently died. Herb's son, Michael, is concerned that Herb will become isolated in his house. Michael wants Herb to move near him, his wife, and Herb's grandchildren. This would mean that Herb would have to give up his home of nearly forty years and move to a strange city. Herb wants to maintain his independence and stay in our community.

What are the needs of this family in terms of the synagogue?

Could the religious school play a role in meeting Herb's needs? Explain.

Scenario D

Melissa and Henry have lived in our community for several years. They have not yet joined a synagogue. Melissa and Henry have come occasionally with friends but are unsure if they can find a place for their family at the synagogue. They are the parents of an eight-year-old daughter, Sarah, who was born with cerebral palsy. Melissa and Henry would like Sarah to have a Jewish education.

What are the needs of this family in terms of the religious school and synagogue?

Text Study

Text 1
Welcoming Guests/Showing Hospitality—*Hachnasat Orchim*

The mitzvah of welcoming guests, hachnasat orchim, *is derived from several stories in the Torah.* Hachnasat orchim *literally means "bringing in of guests," but has come to mean "welcoming the stranger." This mitzvah might also be thought of as showing hospitality to the stranger. In Genesis, Abraham is the first person to perform this mitzvah when he goes out to greet three strangers who pass by his tent: "He [Abraham] said, 'My lords, if it please you, do not go on past your servant. Let a little water be brought; bathe your feet and recline under the tree. And let me fetch a morsel of bread that you may refresh yourselves; then go on—seeing that you have come your servant's way' " (Genesis 18:3–5).*

There is another instance of offering hospitality to a stranger in the book of Genesis. Eliezer, Abraham's servant, is sent on a mission to find a wife for his master's son. On his journey, Eliezer prays for a sign that will tell him he has found the right woman for Isaac. The biblical text reads, "Rebekah . . . came out with her jar on her shoulder. The maiden was very beautiful. . . . [S]he went down to the spring, filled her jar, and came up. The servant ran toward her and said, 'Please, let me sip a little water from your jar.' 'Drink, my lord,' she said. . . . When she had let him drink his fill, she said, 'I will also draw for your camels, until they finish drinking'" (Genesis 24:45–46). The text continues with Rebekah offering food and lodging to Eliezer. After meeting her family, Eliezer offers to take Rebekah back to Isaac as his wife. Due to the hospitality shown to him, Eliezer makes this marriage offer.

Discussion Questions

1. Why would the offer of *hachnasat orchim*, offering hospitality to a stranger, be of such importance in a harsh desert climate, which is the setting of these biblical stories?

2. We may not live in a harsh desert climate, but what parallels can you make between our society today and the biblical world?

3. What did Isaac and Rebekah gain from the Jewish value of offering hospitality to a stranger?

4. In both biblical accounts, hospitality was shown by the offering of food and a place to rest. How would you define hospitality today?

5. What do we gain when we practice the Jewish value of showing hospitality to a stranger?

6. What can our communities gain by welcoming and opening up to newcomers?

Text 2
Loving Your Neighbor—*Ahavat Reiacha*

In the book of Leviticus we read, "You shall love your neighbor as yourself."

(LEVITICUS 19:18)

Many scholars have commented on this mitzvah from the Torah. Rabbi Akiva, a second century Jewish scholar, said that it was the fundamental rule of the Torah. Hillel, a Jewish Sage in the first century C.E.*, wrote this interpretation of it: "What is hateful to you, do not do to others."*

(TALMUD, *SHABBAT* 31A)

Rabbi Moses ben Maimon, also called Maimonides or Rambam, a twelfth-century Sage, taught that we must wish upon others the same degree of success and prosperity we wish upon ourselves and we must treat others with the utmost respect and consideration.

Discussion Questions

1. Which scholarly interpretation of "love your neighbor as yourself" comes closest to your understanding of this mitzvah?

2. What is your personal interpretation of the mitzvah to "love your neighbor as yourself"?

3. In your eyes, what actions, beliefs, and attitudes would fulfill this mitzvah?

Family Discussion: The Mitzvot of Welcoming Guests and Loving One's Neighbor

What is a mitzvah?

The word mitzvah (pl. mitzvot) means commandment or sacred obligation. Sometimes we think of mitzvot as good deeds or Jewish values, but they are more than that. They are commanded behaviors whose source is found in the Torah. It was Rabbi Moses ben Maimon, known as the Rambam, a Jewish scholar of the twelfth century, who found the biblical source for each mitzvah. There are a total of 613 mitzvot, 248 mitzvot that tell us things to do and 365 mitzvot that tell us what not to do. There are mitzvot that tell us how to observe holidays, how and when to pray, what to eat, and how to treat each other. This Family Discussion focuses on the mitzvot of welcoming guests/showing hospitality (*hachnasat orchim*) and loving one's neighbor (*ahavat reiacha*).

Welcoming Guests—*Hachnasat Orchim*

Hachnasat orchim literally means "bringing in of guests," but has come to mean "welcoming the stranger." It may also be thought of as offering hospitality to a stranger. In the Book of Genesis, Abraham welcomes three strangers into his tent, providing them with food and a place to rest. Abraham is the first role model for this mitzvah. The desert is a harsh climate, making survival difficult. Not only did Abraham welcome the strangers, he showed that offering hospitality could save a life.

Discussion Questions

1. Why do you think it is a mitzvah to welcome the stranger and offer hospitality?
2. Have you ever been the new person in class or the new member of a club or group? How did that feel? Did someone make you feel welcome? Who was that? What did that person do?
3. Have you ever welcomed a new person? What did you do?
4. What could you do the next time you meet a new person to make him or her feel more comfortable?

Loving One's Neighbor—*Ahavat Reiacha*

In the Torah it says, "You shall love your neighbor as yourself." The Jewish scholar Hillel said, "What is hateful to you, do not do to others." His words are found in the Talmud. The Ramban, Rabbi Moses ben Maimon, taught that we must wish for others what we would wish for ourselves and we must treat others with the utmost respect and consideration.

Discussion Questions

1. Do you think it is possible to love all our neighbors? How do the words of Hillel and the Rambam help us to understand what this mitzvah requires of us?

2. This mitzvah talks about loving our neighbor. How would you define neighbor? You might think of a neighbor as simply a person who lives near your home. How can you expand that idea and create a bigger definition for "neighbor"?

Imagine

A new family has joined the synagogue. The family includes a mom, a dad, and one daughter. They have come to synagogue occasionally with friends but took a while to decide to join. Their daughter Sarah, who is eight years old, was born with a disease that makes it difficult to walk. She has to wear braces on her legs and she needs to walk with crutches to help her balance. Her parents are hoping that Sarah will be able to make friends at the synagogue and to have a Jewish education. They are unsure about how the other kids and their families will react to Sarah and whether or not their family will feel comfortable at the temple.

Discussion Questions

1. Why do you think it is a challenge for people who are differently-abled to be welcomed and accepted?

2. What is the hardest part of welcoming a new person? What is the best part?

3. How do you think you could help Sarah and her family feel welcome at the synagogue?

4. How could you choose to show love to Sarah and her family?

5. If you followed Hillel's interpretation of *ahavat reiacha*—loving your neighbor—how would you react to Sarah and her family? What if you followed the Rambam's interpretation? Discuss.

6. Which interpretation do you think requires more "mitzvah work"? What do you think the Rabbis would want a person to do? Why?

7. What other things might make someone feel different? How could you help the person feel accepted? When do you feel different? What actions make you feel accepted?

Family Activity Ideas

Mitzvot are Jewish values in action. What can you do to fulfill the mitzvot of *hachnasat orchim* (welcoming the stranger/showing hospitality) and *ahavat reiacha* (loving one's neighbor)?

- Create a family vision statement to which each family member contributes ideas of how the family can foster a warm, loving, and accepting environment in the congregation and general community.
- As a family, make a list of all the good and kind things that can be done when meeting and welcoming a new family to the synagogue. Choose one or two and implement them.
- Make a welcome sign for your home in Hebrew and English, which can read שָׁלוֹם Shalom or בְּרוּכִים הַבָּאִים *B'ruchim Habaim*—Blessed are those who enter.
- Interview a family member or friend who immigrated to this country. Questions to include in the interview:

  How were you welcomed to this country?

  What helped you feel comfortable?

  What do you think new immigrants need?
- Give family members construction paper and ask them to illustrate the mitzvah of welcoming the stranger/showing hospitality or loving one's neighbor. Create a display of these illustrations in your home.
- Host a Shabbat or holiday dinner and invite family, friends, and people you would like to get to know better from the congregation to share in the celebration.
- Learn about and join a committee, group, and/or activity of your congregation to help you build connections with other temple members.

G'milut Chasadim Session 6
Parenting Is *Tikkun Olam*

Introduction

In Judaism, the concept of *tikkun olam* refers to the restoration or repair of an incomplete world. Rabbi Arthur Green writes that "*tikkun olam*, which means 'mending the world,' is an ancient Hebrew phrase that has taken on new life in the past few decades. . . . In contemporary usage it refers to the betterment of the world, including the relief of human suffering, the achievement of peace and mutual respect among peoples, and the protection of the planet itself from destruction."[1]

In this session, participants will consider the possibility of Jewish parenting as *tikkun olam*. They will address the question, "Is it possible to repair our world through the parenting we give our children?"

Enduring Understanding

Nurturing a strong Jewish identity requires the active participation of parents in their children's Jewish living and learning experiences.

Essential Questions

1. Who am I as a Jewish parent and a Jewish role model?
2. How does one establish a sacred relationship between parent and child?
3. What makes a meaningful Jewish life?
4. What does it mean to be a Jewish family?

Questions to Be Addressed

1. What is *tikkun olam*?
2. What does *tikkun olam* have to do with parenting?

---

[1]Arthur Green, *These Are the Words: A Vocabulary of Jewish Spiritual Life* (Woodstock, Vt.: Jewish Lights Publishing, 2000), p. 175.

3. What Jewish values would lead us on the path to see parenting as an opportunity for *tikkun olam*?
4. How do we prepare our children for the world?

Evidence of Understanding

- Participants will share their thoughts, ideas, and opinions on parenting as a way to bring about *tikkun olam*, restoration of the world.
- Participants will apply the concept of *tikkun olam* to their own parenting experiences.
- Participants will take part in creating a graffiti mural that illustrates parenting as *tikkun olam*.

Session Overview

- Set Induction (15–20 minutes)
- The Influence of Parenting (10 minutes)
- Text Study and Discussion (25–30 minutes)
- Graffiti Mural (25 minutes)
- Conclusion (5 minutes)

Materials Needed

- Photocopies of all handouts (pages 193–197)
- Chalkboard and chalk or flip chart and markers
- Containers or baskets for the text slips
- A 6'–10' length of butcher paper labeled "*Tikkun Olam* Is Repairing the World, and Parenting Is *Tikkun Olam* When . . ."

SESSION PLAN

Set Induction (15–20 minutes)

1. Distribute the handouts on pages 193–197. Explain to participants that in Judaism, it is believed that each of us is responsible for making the world a better place for all humanity. The Hebrew phrase for this value is *tikkun olam*. Ask them to refer to Arthur Green's definition on page 193:

   > *Tikkun olam,* which means "mending the world," is an ancient Hebrew phrase that has taken on new life in the past few decades. . . . In contemporary usage it refers to the betterment of the

world, including the relief of human suffering, the achievement of peace and mutual respect among peoples, and the protection of the planet itself from destruction.

Ask participants if this understanding of the term is similar to theirs.

2. Share the midrash on page 194 with the participants. Draw their attention to the phrase at the end of the midrash: ". . . everything that was created during the six days of creation needs finishing: mustard needs sweetening, vetches [green plants] need sweetening, wheat needs grinding, and even man needs finishing." Then discuss the following questions:

   - What do you think it means that each of us "needs finishing"?
   - What tasks face a parent in "finishing" a child?
   - What role do you think Judaism can play in the "finishing" of an individual?

The Influence of Parenting (10 minutes)

1. Ask a volunteer to read the text on page 195 to the entire group:

   > The little world of childhood with its familiar surroundings is a model of the greater world. The more intensively the family has stamped its character upon the child, the more he or she will tend to feel and see its earlier miniature world again in the bigger world of adult life.[2]

2. Pose the following questions for discussion:

   - What do you want to create in the miniature world of childhood for your children that will prepare them for the bigger world of adulthood?
   - When we raise our children with the value of *tikkun olam* (repairing the world), how may that affect their attitudes and behavior when they reach the larger world of adulthood?
   - How is working for a better world an expression of our Jewish values?

Text Study and Discussion (25–30 minutes)

1. Divide the participants into groups of five to seven people. Before the session begins, make one photocopy of the Text Study sheet on pages 196–197 for each group. For each group, cut out each quote and place the slips of paper in a container.

2. On a flip chart or chalkboard write the following questions:

   - What do you learn from this text?
   - How does this text reflect the value of *tikkun olam?*
   - How does this statement apply to Jewish parenting?

---

[2]Carl Jung, *Psychological Reflections: A Jung Anthology* (1953), p. 83.

3. Give a container of text slips to one member of each of the discussion groups. Ask the participant to pull one slip from the container and to read it aloud. The participant is the first to respond to the text using the questions written on the flip chart or chalkboard. The other discussion group participants then express their thoughts.

4. Repeat the process until each participant has a turn to read a text and respond.

5. Reassemble the participants into one large group. Ask each participant to complete the following sentence, sharing their responses aloud:

   My parenting is *tikkun olam* when I ______________________ .

Graffiti Mural (25 minutes)

Participants will create a graffiti mural illustrating the theme "Parenting is *tikkun olam.*"

1. Prepare a long sheet of butcher paper, 6'–10' long. In very large lettering write, "*Tikkun Olam* Is Repairing the World, and Parenting Is *Tikkun Olam* When . . ."

2. Provide the participants with markers in a variety of colors and direct them to respond to the phrase on the butcher paper. Encourage the participants to include drawings, poetry, songs, or any other thoughts or ideas in their responses.

3. If possible, display the graffiti mural in the synagogue.

Conclusion (5 minutes)

Encourage participants to study the Text Study sheet at home. Invite parents to view, read, and discuss the graffiti mural with their children.

Tikkun Olam

Tikkun olam, *which means "mending the world," is an ancient Hebrew phrase that has taken on new life in the past few decades. . . . In contemporary usage it refers to the betterment of the world, including the relief of human suffering, the achievement of peace and mutual respect among peoples, and the protection of the planet itself from destruction.*

(ARTHUR GREEN, *THESE ARE THE WORDS: A VOCABULARY OF JEWISH SPIRITUAL LIFE* [WOODSTOCK, VT.: JEWISH LIGHTS PUBLISHING, 2000], P. 175)

From the Midrash

A pagan philosopher asked R. Hoshaia [Oshaia]: If circumcision is so beloved [of God], why was the mark of circumcision not given to Adam at his creation? R. Hoshaia replied: According to your reasoning, why should a man like you shave the hair of his head [with which he was born], but at the same time leave the adult hair of his beard intact?[1] *The pagan sage replied: Because the hair of his head grew with him in the days of his foolish childhood. Rabbi Hoshaia then argued: If so, he should blind his eyes, lop off his hands, and break his legs, which also grew along with him since the days of his foolish childhood. The philosopher exclaimed: Have we come down to such drivel? R. Hoshaia replied: I cannot let you go without a proper answer. So observe that everything that was created during the six days of creation needs finishing: mustard needs sweetening, vetches [green plants] need sweetening, wheat needs grinding, and even man needs finishing.*[2]

(IN HAYIM NAHMAN BIALIK AND YEHOSHUA HANA RAVNITZKY, EDS., *THE BOOK OF LEGENDS/SEFER HA-AGGADAH*, TRANS. WILLIAM G. BRAUDE [NEW YORK: SCHOCKEN BOOKS, 1992], P. 276)

[1]"Pagan philosophers in Roman times often cut the hair of their head very short but let their beard grow long" (Brother Caedmon Holmes).
[2][*B'reishit Rabbah*] 11:6.

The Influence of Parenting

The little world of childhood with its familiar surroundings is a model of the greater world. The more intensively the family has stamped its character upon the child, the more he or she will tend to feel and see its earlier miniature world again in the bigger world of adult life.

(CARL JUNG, *PSYCHOLOGICAL REFLECTIONS: A JUNG ANTHOLOGY* [1953], P. 83)

Discussion Questions

1. What do you want to create in the miniature world of childhood for your children that will prepare them for the bigger world of adulthood?

2. When we raise our children with the value of *tikkun olam* (repairing the world), how may that affect their attitudes and behavior when they reach the larger world of adulthood?

3. How is working for a better world an expression of our Jewish values?

Text Study

- "When a parent looks at his or her children, the parent's joy makes the parent act like a fool." (*Tanhuma*, *Chayei Sarah*)

- "Childhood is a kind of Paradise." (M. I. Levensohn)

- "For this child I prayed." (I Samuel 1:27)

- "Train up a child in the way he or she should go." (Proverbs 22:6)

- "A child's talk in public comes from either its father or its mother." (Talmud, *Sukkah* 56b)

- "To the one who guides his or her sons and daughters in the right path . . . to that person does the verse apply 'And you shall know that there is peace in your tent.'" (Talmud, *Y'vamot* 62b)

- "As the garden, so the gardener." (*B'reishit Rabbah* 80:1)

- "A parent should never single out one child from the others: because of a scrap of silk of little worth (which made the Coat of Many Colors) Joseph's brothers envied him mortally." (Talmud, *Shabbat*)

- "If we are to achieve a richer culture, rich in contrasting values, we must recognize the whole gamut of human potentialities, and so weave a less arbitrary social fabric, one in which each diverse human gift will find a fitting place." (Margaret Mead)

- "At this very moment we have the necessary techniques, both material and psychological, to create a full and satisfying life for everyone." (B. F. Skinner)

- "In spite of everything I still believe that people are really good at heart." (Anne Frank)

- "I have a dream that my four little children will one day live in a nation where they will not be judged by the color of their skin, but by the content of their character." (Martin Luther King, Jr.)

- "A people without history is like the wind on the buffalo grass." (Sioux saying)

- "A man (or a woman) should never terrorize his (her) household." (Talmud, *Gittin* 6b)

- "If a child is to keep alive his (or her) inborn sense of wonder, he (or she) needs the companionship of at least one adult who can share it, rediscovering with him (or her) the joy, excitement and mystery of the world we live in." (Rachel Carson, *The Sense of Wonder* [New York: Harper & Row, 1956])

- "Words have the power to destroy or heal. When words are both true and kind they can change the world." (Jack Kornfield)